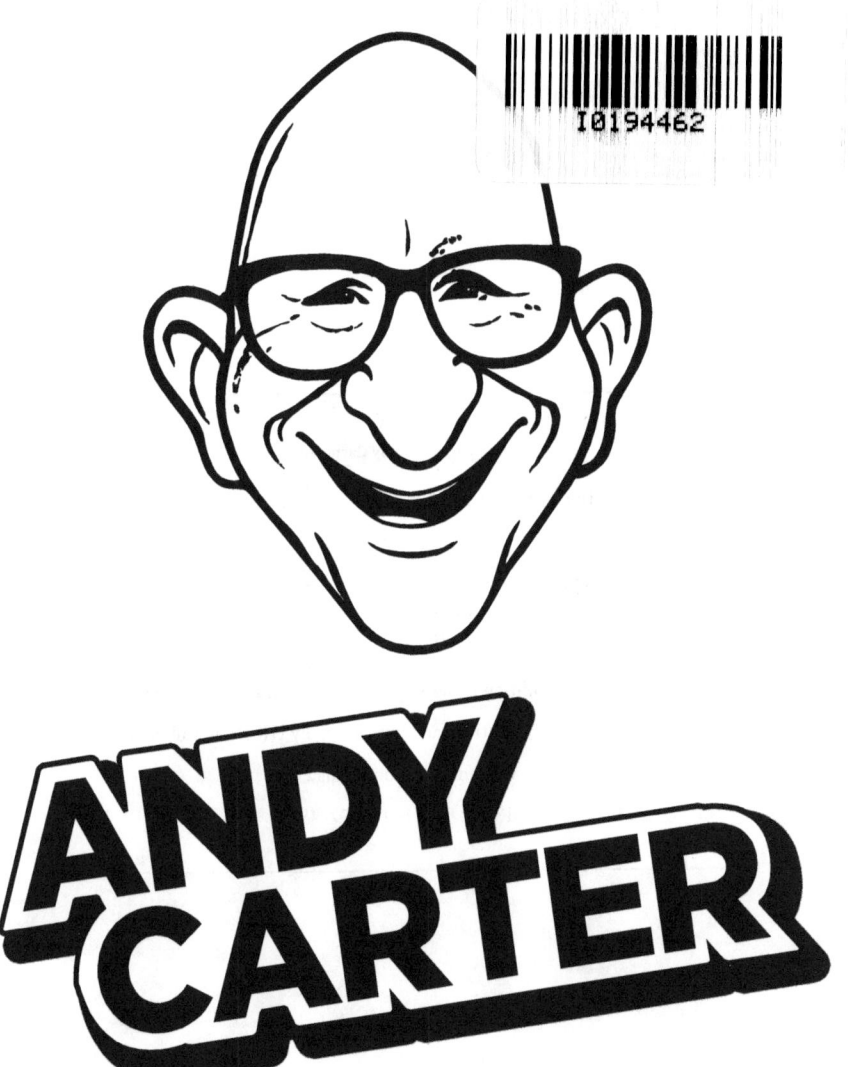

Copyright © Andy Carter 2025

The moral right of this author has been asserted.

All rights reserved.

No part of this publication may be reproduced, stored in a retrieval system, or transmitted, in any form or by any means, without the prior permission in writing of the publisher, nor be otherwise circulated in any form of binding or cover other than that in which it is published and without a similar condition including this condition being imposed on the subsequent purchaser.

Editing, design, typesetting and publishing by UK Book Publishing

www.ukbookpublishing.com

ISBN: 978-1-918077-49-0

CONTENTS

In the Beginning	1
Rhymes and Counting	9
What's in the Salt Pot?	12
Live Sport	16
Miss Jackson	23
Playtime	29
St Andrews and Cubs	36
School Days	42
Rugby The Early Days	49
College	59
Grandparents	64
The Department of Textile Industries	70
Scarred for Life	77
Long Stand	84
All Girls to all Boys	90
Three Days of Hell!	101
Sir, or ADO?	110
The Stick and the Chalk	116
The Norfolk Broads part 1	122
Norfolk Broads Part 2	134
Bullying! What Bullying?	149
Horse Racing, Bookmakers & Gambling	155
Top Banana	161

CONTENTS

The Chocolate Box	166
Blend or Single Malt	172
Public Speaking	177
Desert Island Discs	185
Dead Cats Up Trees	193
The Day Before My Wedding	204
My Wedding Day	208
Exams	217
Fire Heroes... or not?	225
Vinegar, Haggis and Fish	234
The Famous Greenock Morton	239
Age	246
For the Love of Beer!	255
Hornblowers	263
The Speech Which Never was Delivered	269
Drug Smuggler...Me?	277
Golf	283
Dream House	291
Two Hours from Anywhere	301
How Much?	309
Bloody Useless	314
My Opinion of Me	322
Death	334
Eric and the Bottle	341

TO MY MUM AND DAD

Without their encouragement, support and love this
book would never have happened

IN THE BEGINNING

Baildon was the start of a very happy childhood. I was born in November 1961 to Marjorie, a double Olympic gymnast, and Geoffrey, an electrician, and Woodcott Avenue was the first house I remember. It was the family home until June 1968 when we moved to Pudsey. My sister Elaine's arrival had made the family complete nearly four years earlier, in October 1964. The house on Woodcott Avenue was a lovely house, it was semi-detached featuring a through lounge with a coal fire and a large bay window. The kitchen had all the mod cons of the time, gas oven, fridge, top loader washing machine and a huge window looking out over the back garden. Upstairs were three bedrooms, a master bedroom to the front alongside a box bedroom, a large back bedroom which was mine and a bathroom with toilet.

It was in this house Dad and I celebrated my third birthday, just the two of us as Mum was in hospital with Elaine who was receiving treatment for whooping cough. I felt privileged and very special seeing the sandwiches, red jelly and my birthday cake with three candles all laid out on a red Formica kitchen table as Dad was preparing the pending feast. Then we consumed it picnic style off a tea tray with legs in front of the black and white television set. It was on this television I would watch programmes of the time, Casey

Jones, Marine Boy, Blue Peter and Watch with Mother to name a few. In the corner of the large lounge was an old desk bureau, the bottom drawer of which contained all my toys; it was crammed with miniature cars, tractors, lorries and a favourite Greyhound bus.

Woodcott Avenue is a cul-de-sac, but it has a large grass covered roundabout or island in the middle, which was right in front of our house. This is where I learnt to ride my two-wheeler bicycle, Dad running after me as I struggled to keep my balance, after a long apprenticeship using stabilizers. Once I had mastered it there was no stopping me, I was off round and round the island being told I looked like John Surtees, a famous motorbike racer. I was also the proud owner of a gleaming blue and red pedal Go Kart bought from a large bicycle shop in Shipley. This was possibly the best toy ever bought for me.

The island was a great place for the children of the Avenue to play on, and it was easy for parents to keep an eye on us. We spent many a long day playing until our mothers would call us in to get ready for bath time and bed. We played football, cricket and marbles. Emulating our sporting heroes, pretending to be Geoff Boycott or Fred Trueman at Headingley, being Jimmy Greaves as I scored the winner in the Wembley FA Cup final or being Gordon Banks saving a penalty in the last minute to win the game. We loved playing on the island until we heard the loud frightening voice of our nemesis, grumpy old Mr Swan. He would come out of his house and bellow at us to clear off the island. If we tried to stand our ground, he would chase us off and children would scarper in every direction to find refuge in their homes. This put the fear of God into us for a short time until we found the courage to return to the island as Geoff Boycott needed to complete his century and Fred Trueman needed one more wicket to claim a five-for.

At one end of the oval shaped island was a large wooden telegraph pole which was perfect as a pretend set of cricket stumps. On it we would chalk a horizontal line which would represent bails. If the ball hit above this line you were not out, if it hit below the line you were bowled. We also had a two garden and out rule which meant if you hit the ball into a garden on two different occasions in the same innings you were out. This rule did not apply if the ball went into Mr Swan's garden, which was situated right in the path of any half decent on drive, because we were too frightened to try and retrieve it, and it would be confiscated by the tyrant when he discovered it within his rose bushes. This usually meant play was abandoned due to loss of ball, unless of course we found a replacement. Mr Swan must have had a huge stash of different sports balls which may have made the Guinness Book of Records for number of balls in a collection. I can't recall ever getting our balls back and often wonder what the outcome would have been if we'd reported him to the police for theft.

I had a large circle of both male and female friends who lived in the Avenue, so there was always someone available to play with on or around the island. During that period, neighbours were customarily addressed as "Aunty" or "Uncle". I had huge sympathy for one of my favourite aunties, who would spoil me rotten with sweets and treats, as she resided next door to the tyrant Mr Swan. She had a concrete paddling pool in her back garden which from a young child's perspective appeared to be bottomless when in fact it was probably no deeper than three feet, it was seldom full of water, other than rainwater and was usually covered with fallen autumn leaves. On the one occasion I saw it partially filled with 'proper' water was on one hot summer's day, when we were allowed to enter it under supervision; it was very cold, uncomfortable and underwhelming as it was only about ten inches deep, barely reaching my knees, very disappointing to say the least. Looking back, the concrete flagged hole was that big it would have taken days to get the water up to any decent level when trying to fill it just using a garden hose. Other than this one time, we were never allowed anywhere near it when it was empty in case we fell in and hurt ourselves. At the far end of the Avenue, across the island from our house was a snicket leading to an area known as Brook Hill. Brook Hill is a large grassy hillside with a footpath leading to the top which comes out onto Station Road. At this junction was a small corner shop known as Ried's which was full of children's delights, sweets, pop, crisps, lucky bags and comics, plus other commodities of convenience for the local population.

Brook Hill was the scene and start of my lifetime fascination with fire. It was the location where me and a mate, a tall boy with a mass of curly ginger hair, were caught red handed lighting fires and playing with matches. I shudder to think what could have happened if the conditions had been more sympathetic to a naked flame – the whole hillside could have quite easily been engulfed with fire and two small boys stuck in the middle of it all. It didn't feel like it at the time but luckily, we were caught by my friend's mother, who escorted me home and reported the misdemeanour to my mother, who sent me to bed as a punishment. Sent to bed?

Now that was as a six-year-old the hardest and harshest of punishments possible. To be sent to bed in the middle of the day, you may as well send me to prison and throw away the key. Oh, the humiliation!

One year it was decided by my parents to host a family bonfire party at the bottom of the back garden. Watching the bonfire expanding from my bedroom window as chump and wood were added made the excitement and anticipation for the pending event almost unbearable; very little sleep was achieved that week. The day soon arrived, and the fire was lit; it appeared from my junior size to be as big as a block of flats and that hundreds of people were in attendance, when factually it was just a medium sized garden fire with aunts and uncles, both relations and neighbours, in attendance. In the 1960s health and safety was not something that was fashionable or bothered about, resulting in my favourite firework being called the Olympic Torch. This was a handheld firework they gave to me – a five-year-old – which would be a very interesting exercise given today's minefield of restrictions and safety procedures. This small piece of pyrotechnic would spit fire and flame out with frightening force, it was mesmerising and fantastic. I was instructed to hold my arm straight out and rigid, as I pointed it towards a small bund wall approximately five metres away; as I was doing as instructed, unwittingly Mum's twin sister walked right across the line of fire. A shriek and a quick leap over the line of flame helped her avoid any serious injury. Eventually the firework started to burn out into just a yellow flame exiting from its end, so with the fun dissipating I let my arm drop towards my side, but as the laws of physics and fire behaviour dictates, the flame rose up the firework's burnt out tube, over the plastic handle and burnt my hand. It did not burn me seriously, but it did smart and was sore, which made the rest of my evening uncomfortable; health and safety, eh? The food at the party seemed gluttonous, consisting of pie and peas, parkin, toffee, treacle biscuits and home-made toffee apples which was all consumed with great joy as people stood round the controlled inferno of the bonfire at the bottom of our back garden.

Beyond the bottom of the back garden was a smallholding which was owned by an old man called Mr Brown who I never saw without his cloth flat cap, and occasionally we were allowed to go and see all his hens as a treat. One morning as we got up, I heard Dad say to Mum,

"Brown's hens were loud last night; it sounded like they were in our front garden."

Then there was a pause as I heard their bedroom curtains slide open followed by the comment:

"They were on our front lawn!"

What did he mean? I ran into their bedroom to look out of the window to see the lawn strewn with feathers and half devoured hen carcasses. A fox had got into Mr Brown's hens and decided to kill them on our front lawn; the view was one of feather-covered carnage.

Dad would come home from Bradford Power Station where he worked as an electrician, and over dinner, if Mum wasn't coaching in a gym somewhere they would discuss incidents they had experienced throughout their day, Dad mentioning work colleagues by name, and one of these characters was referred to as Frank. Wow what a cool name compared to my plain boring name 'Andrew', how I wished I could change my name to Frank. Weeks later I was playing out as Mum was in the house getting ready to go to work at the gym. As normal when she was ready for me to come in, she stood at the back door calling my name. In the sixties it was commonplace for mothers to stand at the back door calling their offspring at the top of their voices to come home in the knowledge that within a few minutes they would come running. If from a child's point of view, they didn't hear the call, someone would inform them, "Your Mum's been calling for you" to which all entertainment was ceased and off you'd scurry to find out why you were needed. In this instance Mum had apparently called for me two or three times to no avail, I just didn't appear as scripted. So, stage two was to go out and look for me. The next street to Woodcott Avenue is called Mayfield Grove and on the day in question this road was being resurfaced by a gang of road workers. Mayfield Grove was separated from Woodcott Avenue by a wall with a small gap in it to allow pedestrians through but not vehicles. While out looking for me my mother appeared at this gap and asked the workers,

"Have you seen a little boy called Andrew?"

"No missus, sorry," was the reply, so off Mum went to widen the search. Time was passing and the situation was becoming desperate as I could not be found, and Mum could end up being late for work if my appearance was not imminent. My mother's worry of not being able to locate her son was reaching panic stations as other unsavoury scenarios were starting to flow through her mind. Neighbours had joined the search, but this also didn't lead to my discovery, so eventually out of desperation Mum appeared at the gap in the wall to again plead with the road workers,

"Excuse me but are you sure you haven't seen a small, blond haired little boy called Andrew, he is five years old, and we can't find him anywhere."

"No," said the foreman, as they were sat having a tea break. "We only have this little fellow called Frank, who wants to be a road worker for the day." As I leant forward and appeared in Mum's sight with a small sandwich in my hand. The relief on my mother's face was clear for all to see.

"That's not Frank, that's Andrew who I am looking for!"

The relief in her voice and on her face was obvious for all to witness.

The workers apologised for the misunderstanding, and I was marched home by a very relieved parent. At the time, for Mum this was not such a funny incident but like most historical events as time has passed, we have referred to this incident with fondness and amusement.

Woodcott Avenue was clearly a very happy time and place, I had lots of fun and freedom, memories I still look back on with great fondness. It was a very happy time in my life, so when the time came to move on to our new house in Pudsey, it was the saddest day in my six-and-a-half-years of life. I remember leaving, sat in the removal van with tears streaming down my cheeks as I waved goodbye to the best place in the world, in my eyes the centre of the universe. As time moved on all this was soon forgotten as I matured on to bigger and better things, friends and events in Pudsey.

RHYMES AND COUNTING

Around the rugged rock
The ragged rascal ran!
Or as I would say as a three- or four-year-old
Awound the wugged wock
The wagged wascal wan!

Dad would pull his hair out trying to get me to pronounce my 'Rs'. This exercise was often carried out while having my nightly wash in the kitchen sink. I was sat on the draining board totally naked with feet resting in the sink of water while Mum or Dad – mainly Dad – would wash me while reciting rhymes like the one above. I can remember the experience quite well; I remember the extreme cold of the draining board as I lowered my bare bottom onto it, then once this unpleasant experience had passed dipping my feet into the slightly too warm water which was in the sink awaiting the pending ablution. Extreme cold to too hot water as the cold tap was turned on to cool it down to appease shouts of complaint being aired, in those days they did bring us up tough by freezing us then boiling us all within a couple of minutes!

Then the education would start as a soaped-up flannel was ready to wash my body. I remember saying the above rhyme not really understanding what I was saying wrong. As far as my four-year-old brain could understand, I was repeating it word perfect. Dad would cringe with anguish saying "No! Andrew, it's:

> *Arrrround the rrrrugged rrrrock*
> *The rrrragged rrrrascal rrrran!"*

I would slowly mimic rolling my Rs as Dad had demonstrated. The reaction "Yes, yes, Andrew now say it in the rhyme".

> *Awound the wugged wock,*
> *The wagged wascal wan!*

No, no, no! and the process would start over again, until I had been completely washed. As I got older, I began to understand what results Dad was pursuing but this was much later when I was old enough to wash myself, but as a four-year-old I never really understood the problem.

Another exercise we carried out while this washing procedure was being undertaken was to practise my counting. I have been told I could never understand that seven followed six and would insist on replacing it with eleven. I can't recall this happening; it's all down to what I've been told. Apparently, it was another massive frustration for Dad. It would go something like this:

"Right, Andrew, say after me 1,2,3,4,5,6,7,8,9,10."
I would follow:
"1,2,3,4,5,6,11."
"No, no, no, Andrew, 7 not 11."

So off we'd go again, Dad saying 1,2,3,4,5,6,7,8,9,10. Followed by me 1,2,3,4,5,6,11.

"No, no, no!! Seven, seven not eleven, say after me."

Dad 6, me 6, Dad 7, me 7, Dad 8, me 8.

"Right then!" Dad would say believing he had succeeded 1,2,3,4,5,6,7,8,9,10. Followed by me, 1,2,3,4,5,6,11. Argh! No, no, no it's 7, 7 not 11.

This went on night after night, week after week, it must have paid off as eventually I realised that seven followed six not 11. I wish I could remember that Eureka moment when Dad realised it had eventually got through to me.

A lot of learning and parent/son time was experienced while sat on the side with feet in sink and bottom on cold draining board, and it's all remembered with fondness of happy times. Mum and Dad also did this with my sister Elaine. I'm not sure or aware of any education she was given, but I do remember if I stood in the vicinity awaiting my wash and she was trying to wring out the flannel she would flick water all over me as I stood below her feet level in the sink! Fun times and fond memories of a happy childhood. This all happened when we lived in Woodcott Avenue, Baildon, so it was pre-June 1968.

WHAT'S IN THE SALT POT?

We had some good times at Woodcott Avenue, as a family we laugh about many memories from that era. When we left for Pudsey in 1968, I was six years old, and my sister Elaine would have been three and a half. One of these stories is about a teatime incident involving a salt pot.

At Woodcott Avenue we had a kitchen which was separate to a through lounge, and at the rear end of the through lounge was a dining table where we would sit as a family to eat our meals. On the evening in question Dad had made tea, I can't remember what it was, but he had been in the kitchen for some time preparing and cooking the culinary delight. Mum was not present as she was at work in the gym somewhere coaching gymnastics. As the meal preparation was being completed, Dad would be coming in and out presenting the plates of cooked food to the table as Elaine and I sat waiting patiently and with anticipation for our tea. In those days nobody started eating until everyone was sat around the table.

When all plates had been delivered, Dad sat down and all three of us started to eat our meal. On the set table were a tablecloth, knives, forks, salt and pepper shakers both with the same design. They were cone shaped, about six inches high with thin green and white vertical stripes. The salt cellar had a single hole in the top whereas the pepper pot had three – this identified which seasoning was in each of the identical shakers, the two ceramic pieces we had for many years. Having sat down Dad picked up the salt pot to add salt to his meal, but as he shook it he realised nothing was coming out, so he banged the cellar on the table a couple of times to try and dislodge the blockage. He started to shake it over his meal again but to no avail, still no salt was being ejected from the hole in the top of this piece of ceramic. Not to be beaten, he rose from the table and left to go into the kitchen to apply some long thin pointed utensil into the salt pot hole and clear the problem.

On completion of this task he re-entered the dining area, quite quietly I might add, to catch both Elaine and I stood on our chairs, bent over, closely examining the food on Dad's plate. When we saw him, we retreated into our chairs faster than a rabbit going down its burrow, as we wore very sheepish looks on our faces. Unfortunately, we had not been quick enough, and suspicion had been aroused.

"What's going on?" he asked in a low, calm but authoritative tone.

Silence came back at him as his two children looked down at their knees, red faces filled with embarrassment and guilt.

"Well? What's going on?"

"Nothing!" was my reply as three-year-old Elaine's head bowed further.

Once again, quite calmly and in a measured manner Dad said,

"I want to know what's been going on, why were you both looking at my dinner?"

Again, he was hit by a wall of silence.

"Right! You will stay there until one of you explains what has happened and you won't get your dinner until I find out."

At this point we had a scene of a father and his two children sat at a dinner table with the father tucking into his meal and the children sat in silence, their heads bowed, fidgeting nervously, faces awash with guilt, plates full of food in front of them unable to eat their meal. After two- or three-minutes Dad's voice broke the uncomfortable atmosphere.

"Well, are you going to explain yourselves," he demanded between mouthfuls of food. "I want to know what was so interesting about the contents of my plate."

Then after what to me, at six-years-old, seemed like an age of waiting, Elaine, who by this time had tears streaming down her face, confessed the crime.

"Andrew put a bogie in the top of the salt pot, and we were looking to see where it was on your dinner," and that was it.

I scowled at my sister for dobbing me in, but she was only three. Dad was quite calm about it all, he just instructed us to continue eating our dinner, which we did, in total silence. I can't remember any shouting or raised voice, I don't even recall any punishment; he just seemed to accept what had been done, listened to the explanation and was probably dying of laughter inside, while finishing his meal.

I was probably sent to bed early, barred from watching a favourite programme on our black and white TV or not allowed any supper. These were the preferred chastisements of the day, but I can't confirm if any of them were instigated. Across the years since this revolting and disgusting event, we have looked back on it with hilarity and great mirth. Kids! Eh? Dirty little beggers!

LIVE SPORT

I have tried with little success to introduce both my children to live sport. When I was eight, nine and ten years old I would have walked to any sports stadium to see any sort of live sport. Olivia and Alfie have in their time been season ticket holders at Bradford City even though neither had too much interest. Perhaps they attended for my benefit, which I hope is not the case. I would describe it as 'they both went to experience the occasion rather than the event', meaning when we attended home games my friends at the Estonia Club, where we would meet for pre-game drinks, and in the stand at the ground would really make a fuss of them both, but come kick off they would sit there bored out of their brains. Likewise, for away games, we would go on the Shipley Bantams Supporters Club coach, and they were both treated like little stars and royalty, they were the youngest on the bus and would be fully entertained until kick off arrived and once again the boredom would kick in. This for me was frustrating, to say the least!

Dad has told me I sat and watched the 1966 world cup final; I have tried my damnedest but can't remember a single minute of it – I was only four years and nine months old. My first real memory of a live sports game was the 1968 FA Cup Final featuring West Bromwich Albion (West Brom) and

Everton, and I remember West Brom winning 1-0 with a striker called Jeff Astle scoring the winning goal. The same year I remember watching the Rugby League 'watersplash' Challenge Cup Final between Leeds and Wakefield Trinity when the unfortunate Don Fox missed a last-minute conversion, right in front of the posts which would have won them the game, my first experience of witnessing sport disappointment and how cruel it can sometimes be. I don't remember much about the 1969 cup final between Leicester and Manchester City, but the 1970 final is a different story. By 1970 I was a big Leeds United fan. Allan Clarke, the Leeds striker, was my boyhood footballing hero. When I discovered his initials were the same as mine, A.J.C., I was the happiest boy on the planet. I can remember the game vividly, the sandy pitch, Jack 'the Giraffe' Charlton scoring the opening goal, Eddie Grey down the left wing, Peter Houseman's first equalising goal when Gary Sprake messed up, Mick Jones re-establishing the lead and in the last few minutes feeling gutted when Chelsea equalised again, my first experience of overwhelming disappointment due to sport. This all led to a replay at Old Trafford later that week, a game Leeds lost. It was a midweek fixture, so I was only allowed to watch the first half due to bedtime and although I was unhappy the following morning when I found out the score, 2-1 to Chelsea, it didn't have any real emotion attached as I hadn't witnessed it for real. This game has since been described as the most brutal and dirty football match ever to be played in England which, as a nine-year-old I was totally unaware of this impact till later years.

    This football match, or saga, fuelled my appetite for football, and later that year was the 1970 World Cup Finals in Mexico, which I couldn't get enough of watching. Seeing the Brazilians with names like Pele, Jaizinho, Revellino, Tostao and Carlos Alberto, and their goalkeeper's name was Felix which I found very amusing as in my mind Felix was a cartoon cat. West Germany with Maier, Beckenbauer, Muller and Seeler broke our hearts by gaining revenge for 1966 and knocking England out in the quarter finals, another heartbreaking experience which became a feeling I would have to get used to over the coming years, as sport, I soon discovered, can be very cruel. I did watch the World Cup Final of 1970, contested between Brazil and Italy, Brazil winning 4-1. I loved the whole tournament, football on the black and white television, every day. I had posters on my bedroom wall, Esso petrol garages gave England coins away with fuel purchases of which Dad managed to get me a full set; I also had hats, scarves and rosettes. I became a proper little England fan, in all the sports I follow, which has lasted till this day.

Later in that year, 7th November 1970, yes, my 9th birthday, I was taken to Headingley for my birthday treat, to watch the Rugby League World Cup Final, Great Britain v Australia; this was my first experience of attending a live sports event, and a World Cup Final to boot. This got me instantly hooked on live sport, everything about it was brilliant, the buzz and hum of the crowd of 19,000, the noise, the colours and the atmosphere, all of it! After the disappointment – yet another, with Australia beating Great Britain 7-12 – we made our way home across the cricket field, where it was explained to me that we were tracing the steps of some of the world's all-time great cricketers. The names of Bradman, Hutton, Sutcliffe, Hammond, Benaud,

Trueman and Boycott, all who had graced that very same pitch. Players I had only heard of or seen on television – as a small boy I had listened in awe, and fascination, mesmerised by the stories of these great cricketers, the feeling I had while walking across this hallowed turf was quite intoxicating and overwhelming.

After this first experience all I wanted to do was experience live sport, I needed more of this newfound exhilarating experience, any sport with a large crowd would fulfil the craving. Live sport had a unique buzz that was far more exciting than watching it on television. I craved to attend on a regular basis, Leeds United would be perfect, but it wasn't to be, I was too young to go on my own and no one was able to take me. When I spoke to my fellow peers in the Junior School playground, who were taken to Elland Road by their parents, about that weekend's fixture, I was quite envious. My appetite for live sport flourished, so when we got our first colour television for Mum to watch the 1972 Olympic Games in Munich, it was the new best day of my life, the ability to see all this sport in full colour could only add to my thirst for more, even though it still didn't compare to attending events. Watching Rugby, The Lions and Five Nations, Football, including FA Cup Finals, Cricket test matches and one-day competitions were unmissable; of course this was long before 'pay a fortune TV', when all sport was screened on terrestrial television channels and was accessible to everybody.

My 11th birthday arrived in November 1972 and in commonplace with family tradition I was due a birthday surprise and treat. I knew it was coming but didn't know what it was or where I was going. It usually involved a trip to the cinema or a meal out but when I asked if these were possibilities I was told 'No!'. Here comes the big disappointment, for something which would be the best treat ever. While trying to guess what my surprise would be I came up with many plausible ideas, all of which received a negative response, until I asked with no expectation,

"Tickets to go see Leeds United at Elland Road?" to which the reply was, "Yes!".

Wow! I was ecstatic, but I wish they had maintained the surprise. Why did they have to say yes? Perhaps it was to stop my nattering, perhaps it was the honesty, but by saying yes and accepting my guess was correct caused a great deflation within me; this nearly, but didn't spoil the day. It is said you always remember your first football game, and I do, 11th November 1972, Leeds United v Sheffield United at Elland Road. Leeds won 2-1 with goals from Allan Clarke, my hero, and Peter Lorimer, with the Sheffield United's goal scored by Tony Currie. The day was brilliant, once again the sounds, colour and atmosphere got my juices flowing, so here's to many more – but they never came, well it wasn't my birthday every Saturday, was it?

A year later, one Sunday some friends of my parents called in to see us on their way to watch Bradford Northern v Huyton at Odsal Stadium. It was Sunday 18th November 1973. As I listened into the conversation, I heard myself say, "Can I come to the match with you?"

After being told off for being cheeky – well, if you don't ask you don't get, the friends said, "Yes, you can if you want".

That was it, that was the start of my love affair with Bradford Northern RL and regular live sport. These friends along with their son ended up taking me to the majority of

Bradford Northern games home and away for the rest of the seventies and into the early eighties, they took me to every rugby league ground in the country, north to Barrow and Workington, east to Hull and Hull KR, west to St Helens and Widnes, and south to Doncaster and every club in between.

Bradford Northern was my passion, I held a schoolboy pass each year which cost the princely sum of one pound; this was basically a junior season ticket which allowed entry to every home game. My life revolved round Bradford Northern, I had many scarves, hats, rosettes and even a rattle, and would be draped in the colours at all games I attended. For special fixtures, specifically Challenge Cup games, I would be given an old policeman's helmet painted white with a single red, yellow and black hoop circling it. Wearing it was quite the novelty and talking point among supporters of both teams who would smile and comment on it. I loved to wear the helmet and be centre of attention, so much so that I did the same many years later with one of my old fire helmets. My enthusiasm and support for Bradford Northern and the live matches knew no limits, to such an extent their name was plastered all over my exercise books. The name, slogans, even crowd scenes were all drawn on the covers and inside pages. Dad stated later that if I'd "spent as much time" on my studies as I did write "Bradford Northern" on my books, I would have been "a genius".

I ceased watching Bradford Northern in the early 1980s, just after Peter Fox, another of my sporting heroes had led them as coach to the league title for the second year in a row. There were a few reasons why I stopped going to Odsal, but the main one was finance, or lack of it. I was now too old to qualify as a schoolboy and had to find my own money for a season ticket, about £45. This was not easy on a Junior Technician's pay so I tried to attend each Sunday and pay on the gate, but finding the £5 admission and bus fare each week was not at that time a priority. This is when I discovered Bradford City. Don't ask me which was the first game I attended, but I can tell you how it all started. In 1981 I was Playing Rugby for the Phoenix Park Colts and after training one evening as we were getting dressed, one of the lads said, "Bradford City are playing tomorrow night; shall we all go?"

That evening marked the beginning of my enduring passion for the Mighty Bantams, which has continued for over forty years. The days of Leeds United had long been forgotten as a decade of rugby league had diluted any interest in football until this date. They do say you can change your house, change your car, even change your wife but you never change your football team. Well, I am an example of an exception to the rule as I did change my football team.

Even now I have a thirst and craving for any live sport ranging from Junior Rugby, Football and Cricket at the local parks and clubs, Bradford City home and away, Horse Racing meetings, Cricket and Rugby Union club and international games. The only problem with the latter two is cost of tickets can sometimes be unjustifiable, and I cannot afford a monthly subscription to satellite, cost a fortune, TV so I must make do with what our budget can substantiate. Nevertheless, my passion and thirst for live sport is relentless and intoxicating, a sentiment which remains with me till this day. Live sport, bring it on!

MISS JACKSON

Something was said today which reminded me of Miss Jackson. Miss Jackson was a short rotund, elderly lady, well from a nine-year-old's perspective appeared elderly. Who was Miss Jackson? I hear you ask. Miss Jackson was a schoolteacher who taught me in the third year at Waterloo Junior School on Victoria Road in Pudsey. She had a reputation for being very strict and frightening to all pupils who crossed her path.

When we moved from Baildon to Pudsey in 1967, I was sent to Waterloo Infants School on Waterloo Road. This school was linked to the junior school, but they were two separate buildings about three hundred yards apart. When I left the infant school, I was passed through natural progression up the road to the juniors. In my first year I was in Mrs Chater's class, in the second year Miss Smith who got married and became Mrs Greenbank. Towards the end of the school year and every year for that matter we were told whose class we would be in the following year, starting in September after the school six weeks holiday. The third-year teachers were Mrs Archer, a lovely lady with a kind, pleasant reputation and the tyrant known as Miss Jackson whose fearsome reputation was well known.

THE WORLD ACCORDING TO ANDY CARTER

There were rumours about a boy who was a school year above me in Miss Jackson's class when I was in Mrs Greenbank's class. This guy had quite long hair which most youths did in the early 1970s, he had a fringe which would fall over his eyes. This was like a red rag to a bull; his fringe hanging over his eyes must have irritated Miss Jackson so much she got hold of a girl's hair clip and clipped his hair back out of his eyes and made him sit there in humiliation at his desk all day wearing it. He was told he would have to keep the clip in every day until he'd had his hair cut. How embarrassing was this for a young juvenile male being made to sit in a class with a girl's clip in his hair? Stories like this and others involving chalk and board rubbers being launched across the classroom with laser guided precision with high velocity toward any child who had the audacity to step out of line absolutely terrified me.

With all this in mind as the second year progressed, realisation kicked in and I was soon to work out that the following year I would either be in Mrs Archer's class or unthinkably Miss Jackson's class. As the date loomed nearer and nearer for the great announcement, I prayed every night that the good lord would see it in his wisdom to put me into Mrs Archer's class. In 1971, every child in the second year would go to bed reciting the same prayer. None of them wished to be placed in Miss Jackson's class. The day came, the penultimate day before the long awaited six weeks summer holiday we were told who would be joining which third year class the following term. Sure enough, I got Miss Jackson, huh yet another reason to doubt the existence of a god. Well, when I got the news, I was distraught, my heart not only sank, it fairly plummeted into my socks. The feeling of devastation consumed me, for a young nine-year-old this was not an overreaction it was the worst possible thing that could have happened. How could anyone with any inkling of child protection allow me to go into Miss Jackson's class? Some of my friends obviously suffered the same fate and would join me, which reduced the psychological blow slightly, but would we be able to talk to each other, see each other, sit next to each other and watch each other suffer the wrath of the tyrant called Miss Jackson? The fact some of my peers were joining me in the dark chasm of the classroom run by this monster of a human being through the eyes of a nine-year-old didn't really help my situation, the bottom line was it was I, yes me! who was going into this class and it was me who was going to experience this imagination-fuelled awfulness. Other friends who had been sent to Mrs Archer's class had broad grins on their faces and made it known at every available opportunity how grateful they were that they'd dodged a bullet.

The six-week holiday helped to take my mind off the pending doom but as we got nearer the fateful day the nerves, fear and dread became stronger and stronger. On the day we returned to school I asked Mum and Dad if I could take a bouquet of flowers for Miss Jackson, well anything to appease the tyrant and soften the blow. I was desperate!! Unfortunately, my request was denied, probably a good thing really as I could have been a bit of a laughingstock among my classmates. The answer to my request was 'Don't be silly!' – it was ok for parents to say that they weren't about to enter Miss Jackson's class, or more to the point the jaws of hell!!

But Miss Jackson turned out to be the best teacher I ever had all the way through my schooling. Yes, she was strict which as nine- and ten-year-olds we probably needed, but she was also very fair. Each week two fourth year pupils would call on each class to count house points and check the classes' attendance records. There were four houses at the school, Australia (Red), Canada (Blue), New Zealand (Green) and West Indies (Yellow). Students were awarded house points for good work and good behaviour. Miss Jackson would allow the fourth years to enter the classroom and they would make note of the house points which were by the door, written on the right-hand corner of the blackboard which stretched the whole length of the classroom. On each Friday the school would hold a large assembly, which each class would attend. As the pupils walked into the school hall all eyes were raised to a big colourful board displaying the four houses. The name of each house was on sliding wooden slats which would be placed in order first, second, third and fourth; this was the result of all the house points gathered by the two fourth year pupils. Also, and by far the most important, was the class which had achieved the best attendance throughout the week, because if your class number was written up there on the board alongside the percentage gained it meant your class was rewarded ten minutes' extra playtime on the break of the class's choice the following week. Miss Jackson never failed, she would ask us which day we would prefer and which break, morning or afternoon. If on the chosen day the weather was inclement, we could move it to a more suitable day and if in her view the class had behaved well that week she would allow us an extra five minutes on top of the ten minutes bonus. I can still see her now patrolling up and down the long corridor parallel to the playground keeping her eye on us but also keeping her distance.

One morning we awoke to thick snow. In those days the schools were kept open, not like now when one flake falls the schools shut. I remember Mum making us go to school. The snow was deep and thick and the walk to school was magical, I played in it with other children on the way. Snowballing, sliding, snow angels, and the odd sledge appeared; it was all great fun. When I arrived, the class was half empty as a lot of my fellow pupils had not bothered attending. The following day when the conditions were more manageable and slightly improved, the absentees from the previous day returned. Miss Jackson was not happy – perhaps she knew our attendance record was shot for that week. She confronted the previous day's missing pupils.

"Where were you all yesterday?" She barked. "A bit of snow! Where were you?"

A few excuses and justifications followed none of which seemed to satisfy Miss Jackson. Then she picked on the girl sat next to me.

"Where were you, Sharon Ball?"

"We couldn't get in and thought the school would be closed," she answered timidly.

"Couldn't get in? Couldn't get in?" Miss Jackson boomed. "You got in, didn't you, Andrew Carter?"

I sat upright at the unexpected mention of my name. "Y, yes Miss," I stuttered.

"How?" she demanded.

"I walked in, Miss."

"Walked in, he walked in," she repeated, "and Andrew Carter lives further away from school than you, doesn't he, Sharon Ball?"

I was ten years old; I remember feeling ten feet tall as my chest expanded with pride, I had pleased Miss Jackson, all my best days had come at once and for a split second she may have actually loved me! Wow! What a feeling.

I did feel a bit sorry for Sharon Ball though, because at the age of ten it was hardly her sole decision whether to attend school that day or not, her parents would have had the ultimate input into that decision. Miss Jackson had her moments, but I loved being in her class, all the worry over the preceding six-week holiday was stress I didn't need, nor should I have been so concerned and frightened. This was a great early lesson for me to judge people as you find them and not on reputation or other people's opinions. She was brilliant, the best teacher I've ever had! It's just a shame in my eyes there doesn't seem to be teaching of that calibre today, and her secret was simple DISCIPLINE which seems to be in short supply with the current generation. So, here's to Miss Jackson R.I.P.

.

PLAYTIME

I sometimes look at the young generation of today and think how much they have missed out on. Yet in their eyes they don't understand how my generation managed with no smartphone, computer games, internet and social media, or multi-channel TV. So how did we entertain ourselves when none of the above were available? We only had three TV channels to choose from and not a lot of that was child friendly.

As children walked to Junior school any observant bystander would notice most of the boys carrying a cloth bag held by a drawstring. This bag would be full of marbles, glass spheres with coloured centres. Each marble would be highly polished and ready for playtime's enthusiastic competition. Holes in the turfed ground would be made by twisting the heel of a child's shoe round and round. Then two, three or four boys would stand behind a mark and throw their marbles toward the hole. Marbles on the ground surrounding the hole would be projected towards the target using the upper part of the index finger. If the participant missed, the turn was passed on to the next player, this process would continue until all live marbles were resting in the hole. Whoever sunk the last marble won and retained the hole's contents. This meant marble collections could grow and diminish at equal rate depending on the individual's success or failure. Some boys had larger oversized marbles which were worth two of the standard size, known as twoers, and occasionally a bolly (ball bearing) would be involved.

From memory marbles was mainly a male game, the females would be in their area of the playground with tennis balls knotted into the end of an old stocking. The stocking would have a loop tied into the opposite end and placed round the ankle of one leg, then using centrifugal force the weighted ball would be sent round in circles while the other leg would skip over as it passed. Skipping with a rope was also considered a girl's game. Some would skip all the way to school. On arrival the skipping ropes would be opened out with a twirler at each end while the rest of the friendship group would time a run and jump over the twirling rope. This would be done in ones, pairs and even threes dependent on the number participating. Some girls would have a whip and top. This consisted of a wooden pointed top which was set off spinning, the girls would whip it to death holding a short stick with a leather string pinned to one end to maintain the rapid revolutions of the top.

When the months of September and October arrived the drawstring bag of marbles would be replaced by conkers on a string. These seeds of the horse chestnut tree would be eagerly gathered by children each evening and weekend. If they hadn't yet fallen, branches, sticks, stones and other objects would be launched into the leafy canopy to try and dislodge any visible large nuts. Every playtime would hold the mythical 'Conker World Championships' – well it was in an eight-year-old's mind. Each conker was classified depending on how many it had defeated previously. Every brand-new conker started as a 'noner', when two noners had a conker duel the winning conker would become a oner and so on. Using this method of counting, an individual conker could get up to the hundred plus quite easily. If one participant for example had a fifty-twoer and he lost to a tenner, the winning conker would suddenly become a sixty-twoer. This method, accepted as it was, was open to juvenile exaggeration, but most of the time the number stated on each conker was acknowledged as true. One boy would stand, still as a statue, holding up his stringed conker ready for his opponent to strike it with his conker. If a player hit the conker, he would take another turn. If he missed, the roles would be reversed until one of the conkers split and came off the string. Excited voices would claim, clench (strings tangled), stamps (as a conker fell off the string it could be stamped on) or tibs (a glancing connection between the two nuts).

Other school playtime entertainment would include football, cricket and tig. Bouncy balls also held children's attention, the hardened rubber compound balls had a very exaggerated bounce which would be fired across the playground and chased. The only problem was because of the huge bounce, the control of the balls could prove difficult and consequently numerous balls were lost over walls, down roads and into gardens. Hoopla, hopscotch, 'What time is it, Mr Wolf', and a game involving bunny hops, backward steps, fairy steps and lamp posts, the title of which escapes me, were other playground activities performed by children.

Away from school, children's entertainment was altogether different, mainly due to there being no playground perimeter, the vast outdoors was endless. The only restriction being parental instruction demanding you didn't stray too far. Consequently, most playing hours would be spent using wheeled equipment. Bicycles, scooters, skateboards, roller skates, and home-made bogies were all used hour after hour. If you were lucky enough to live on a hill, even better. The laws of gravity and physics allowed less physical exertion and more freewheeling while you sat back and enjoyed the ride. Street games without wheels would include 'Kick Can and Hop-it', though unlike the name suggests it was usually a football rather than a can used. A member of the gang would kick the ball as far away as possible, while the seeker absconds to retrieve it, the rest of the players would scatter and hide. On return the seeker would place the ball back on the spot and search for the hidden friends. If he or she left the vicinity of the ball for too long, the hidden could sneak out of their cover and kick the ball away. This would release any individuals already caught and the process would start again. Not until the ball was on its spot with all escapees caught would the game be over. The game could last for hours until boredom set in. Where I lived there was a cow field behind the house which was used on a windy day for kite flying. One child would get a newly purchased kite flying and within an hour there could be up to half a dozen others doing the same thing.

In winter, snowballing, sledging, and sliding were the order of the day. Any individual could only join in on a nurtured and well looked after slide if they had tread-less shoes on. One person would stand at the start of the slide checking shoes for worn soles, then making the decision whether you were allowed to slide. Sledging was the most popular winter pastime. After a large deposit of snow, the usual green, grassy banks or fields would be descended on by hundreds of children of all ages including parents too. The incline in front of you would be turned into an amateur version of the Cresta Run. The descent was usually exhilarating but every positive has a negative, the trudge back up the hill through deep snow was the gruelling energy sapping downside. Small children were hauled back up to the summit sat on the sledge, while slightly older children could be seen in tears, wet and cold at the bottom of the hill with the oppressive prospect of the long climb to be conquered before another speed induced slide could begin. Snowballs would be thrown when snow had fallen. At the sledging site, on the way to school and in the playground. Mass snowball fights involving large numbers were common at school. The pupils would part, and the skies would be filled with snowballs being launched from one side to another.

If the weather was inclement, inside entertainment was the order of the day. Occasionally in the school holidays there may be up to four friends in one house, but the more usual case was you on your own or with a sibling or two. Wooden cotton bobbins were used as a good source of entertainment. Making a cotton bobbin tank which involved a wooden bobbin with notches cut into the rim, a matchstick, a small piece of candle wax and a rubber band. The rubber band was threaded through the bobbin and candle wax attached to a long matchstick. The matchstick would be wound up twisting the rubber band then let go. As the rubber band unwound, the bobbin would move forward, hence the name Cotton Bobbin Tank. Also, there was cotton bobbin knitting. Children would spend hours threading wool round four nails which had been tapped into the bobbin around the hole. Eventually a tail of thin knitted wool would emerge from the bottom of the bobbin. Hours were spent competing to see who could achieve the longest tail. This simple but effective activity could entertain youths for hours. Board games, jigsaws and puzzles were other forms of wet weather entertainment. Hours even days of competitive Monopoly, Go for Broke, Hotel, Risk (for older kids), Popstars or Polyeconomy would pass the wet hours away.

Whenever the weather was good, and the schools were on vacation, the streets were a noisy place filled with young people's excited chatter, laughter, shouts and screams. Today we seem to have lost this environment. Children of today don't seem to play out like they used to. No longer is there Cowboys and Indians with toy guns and bows and arrows. No hide and seek, no street football or cricket and no bike riding. This results in most of today's streets and cul de sacs being very quiet with a library-like environment. I get the fact that today's society may be perhaps more dangerous and the safety of our young should never be compromised, but surely this isn't the only reason. From as early as eight years old I was trusted to walk to and from school with mates of comparable age. Nowadays most children are either driven there or escorted on foot by adults. Internet and gaming seem to keep children locked away in their rooms, I accept they interact with their friends online and if they are upstairs parents at least know there whereabouts, which is a good thing. I do, however, feel we have lost something. Being outside and hearing parents calling from their doorstep for their offspring to come home as it's bathtime is a sound I fear society has lost. Being told as a child: "Your mum's been calling you" is a statement few of today's children have ever used. As previously stated for me, well I feel we have lost something. While internet, games, and smartphones have their place, surely outdoor activities in the fresh air must be a far better environment for children?

ST ANDREWS AND CUBS

Arriving in Pudsey in 1968 Elaine and I were sent to Sunday School every Sunday morning at St Andrew's Methodist Church. We were often sent to church by ourselves, Mum was usually coaching at the gym, while Dad would drop us off at the church side door and pick us up from the same place when the service and Sunday school had concluded. Never in my memory did he ever come inside, as far as we knew he was at home preparing that day's Sunday dinner; I think looking back this may just have been a convenient babysitting service. I attended Sunday School until I was 15 when I discovered Colts under 19s rugby at Bingley Rugby club. It was one of my short life's major surprises when I informed my parents, I didn't want to attend church anymore and would prefer to play rugby instead. Surprisingly they didn't question why or give reasons why I shouldn't give up attending church, they just accepted my decision which was met with very little resistance.

One positive which came out of attending St Andrew's was being asked if I wanted to join the 4th Pudsey cub scouts. I said I did, not really understanding what this entailed, but every fourth Sunday I would be sat in church at the Family Service, not that my parents were there, and observe the cubs, scouts, brownies and guides parade their flags and colours in the church. Watching this colourful procession looked very much like something I would like to be involved in, so for this sole reason I joined the cubs in 1970. The cub leader or Akala was a lovely man who ran a good active pack. He was joined not long after I started by a lady assistant, known to us boys as Baloo, who mothered us all. I stayed in touch with her for much of her life and cleaned her windows in my window cleaning days. Pack night was on a Thursday evening; it would typically start with the Grand Howl. Akala would shout 'Pack! Pack! Pack!' and all cubs would stop what they were doing and congregate in a circle around him in the middle of the room. Akala would then stretch his arms out horizontally, then lower them down by his side which was the cue for the cubs to crouch down and chant,

"Akala! We'll do our best!" then all the boys would stand up to attention as the duty sixer, who was facing Akala, would shout,

"Cubs do your best!" to which the rest of the pack would reply,

"We will do our best," and then all saluted as Akala returned the salute. Then the duty sixer would leave the circle and head to the rolled-up Union Flag, break it, stand back and salute it as the rest would follow suit.

After grand howl and flag break, we would play some sort of game, whack 'em, Keys or other similar games, followed by a badge work activity, working on achieving one of the three arrow badges Bronze, Silver or Gold, or it could be specific work for one of the many proficiency badges. The proficiency badges were my favourite; I loved the challenges they would bring and by the time I graduated into scouts I had achieved an armful. We'd break for a cup of orange juice and a biscuit followed by another game. The evening would then close with a final grand howl, prayers, notices, flag down then home. I went to cubs each week armed with an old sixpence in my pocket; this was the value of two and a half pence after decimalisation. The sixpence paid one penny for subs, half penny for orange juice and biscuit and one penny for a bag of chips with scraps from the Lidget Hill fish and chip shop on the way home. I can still remember the smell of fish and chips, salt and vinegar as we entered the shop, it was such an inviting and comforting aroma.

When we were eight to ten years old, my friends and I would walk home alone from cubs in Pudsey, even in the dark winter months; it was a journey of over a mile, which seems unlikely in today's less safe society. It appeared we were given a lot more responsibility at a far younger age. We were in a group of three or four, chips were bought at Lidget Hill and as we ate them, we would walk the length of Cemetery Road, past the graveyard, spooky, then up Owlcotes Road, dropping members at their homes as we passed. Occasionally we would take an alternative route and head through Pudsey centre, up past the old police station then down through the secluded ginnel onto Waterloo Road then up Sunnyridge Avenue. I can clearly remember passing Waterloo Post Office under a cloudless, star-filled sky, looking to see if we could see the lost spacecraft and astronauts of the Apollo 13 mission, the minds and imagination of eight-year-old boys. This was April 1970, a month before Leeds United played Chelsea in the FA Cup final of that year, and Gay Trip won the Grand National that month, two sporting events I followed avidly.

We enjoyed many outdoor activities with 4th Pudsey cubs, mainly on a weekend with small hikes on Ilkley Moor or more local walks to Tong and back. We would make plastercasts of animal footprints, light small fires to toast marshmallows, boil water for cups of tea or simply brush up our compass and map reading skills. The biggest adventure was a joint week away with 2nd Calverley cubs to Snowball Plantation at York. The 2nd Calverley leader was an elderly chap, and their pack was full of great lads, who all became good mates throughout that week. Snowball Plantation is a hostel type building in an open space in the middle of a large wood. We had a fantastic week of activities, including trips into York, swimming, bivouac building, cowboy and Indian games in the woods. The woods opened themselves up to multiple activities of hide 'n' seek in the daylight hours and spotlight at night. The obligatory campfires were held with singsongs and sketches. These campfires were fantastic, and I loved them, everyone singing funny entertaining songs, leaders dressed and draped in their campfire blankets, a feeling of glow and warmth of the fire on my face, yet the cold and shiver of the night down my back, oh happy memories. I used these experiences in later years when I became a leader, hoping my scouts would get the same joy and awe at the campfires I would run. It was a great week which was my first experience of being away from home, the first of many scouting activities I attended and eventually organised.

Another cub activity which would fill me with pride was on the last pack meeting before church parade on the Sunday, at flag down Akala would pick a cub to be flag bearer and two others to be escorts. Being picked as an escort was good, but to be picked to carry the flag was off the scale, a phenomenal feeling. The pride when your name was called was chest bursting. If picked you would be given the flag to take home and polish the brasses. The flag was yellow, displaying the large green cub scout emblem of three feathers in the centre and supporting a brass fleur-de-lis on the top of the pole. On arrival at church on the Sunday morning wearing immaculate uniform, which consisted of cap, green cub jumper with badges stitched on, an ironed and neatly rolled light blue necker, held together by a coloured woggle representing the colour of your six, grey shorts, grey socks with green garter tabs exposed from under the roll tops and highly polished shoes. After passing the smartness test, which to my knowledge no one ever failed, we were lined up outside church with the cubs and scouts up one side of the step and the brownies and guides up the other side.

When the service began, we would be led into church with the leaders instructing us to lower the flags so they didn't collide with the overhanging balcony, which would cause the worst case of embarrassment if you forgot. As we walked down the two aisles, guides down one side and scouts down the other, the escorts would stop at the end of the first pew while the flag bearers would continue to the front and present the colours to the minister. St George's flag first, the scout flag second and finally the cub flag. When you had progressed into scouts to be asked to carry the St George's flag was the ultimate accolade. As the service was concluding, and the final hymn was being sung, the whole process would be repeated in reverse.

That was the start of my long scouting career where I was taught principles, respect and discipline which I have endeavoured to follow throughout my life. I remember these times as happier and simpler times where attention to detail, discipline, and pride all mattered, whereas today I feel these values are in short supply. Due to the change in structure and the sense of freedom, I don't think the Scouting Association is the same now compared to what it was then. Health and safety got involved – which is not a bad thing but on occasions I think it can be restrictive – smart uniform was changed to sweatshirts and jeans, females were allowed to join when in my mind they had the Guide Movement – this causes problems in leadership recruitment as you need female leaders for female scouts, and the badge system became a free for all. These changes were implemented to try and make the scout movement more popular with the youth of the day, when in fact it turned into just another glorified babysitting youth club. I am of the opinion, if it isn't broke don't try and fix it. And it wasn't broke!!

SCHOOL DAYS

When I talk about my school days, I am usually referring to my time as a pupil at Pudsey Grammar School (PGS) from September 1973 to June 1978. I don't really know whether I didn't like school or just school didn't like me. Looking back, I don't think I was a very mature student, but then again what teenager is? We were taught in a world of discipline involving detentions, canings and other forms of physical pain. I often wonder if I'd attended school currently, with seemingly no or very little discipline and with children apparently in control, whether I'd have performed better or worse. In my time we had some teachers who were rather nasty pieces of work. One of my schoolgirl colleagues who to this day, 47 years later, still hates her time at PGS and tells tales of how teachers belittled and bullied her mentally because she may not understand subjects taught. Being referred to as thick, stupid, idiotic, daft or simple did not help to promote inspiration or motivation. Teachers were there to teach and not intimidate.

I can't say I was never bullied by teachers, but I was hardly a model student either. I attended classes because I had to, left them when they'd finished because I could, and promptly forgot most things taught and explained to me in the previous hour; I couldn't get out to see my mates quick enough. I would mess about during lessons trying to be the joker. I wouldn't describe my behaviour as bad or even disruptive, more mischievous with never any malice in any of my actions. I was the class clown, others would come up with daft ideas and I would be the fool to carry them out, all because of my craving to be accepted and I enjoyed the laughter these small childish stunts would bring my way.

I did enjoy Physical Education (PE) and because of Mum's Olympic history I think the PE teachers liked me. I always received good report marks from PE which when pointed out to my parents after achieving more than one substandard school report didn't wash or ease their disappointment. They would say, "Being good at PE isn't going to get you a job, is it?" In my latter years of school I did represent Pudsey Grammar School as first team goalkeeper, laughable now due to my lack of inches, first team wicketkeeper, basically because I had my own wicketkeeping gloves, well Dad's really old gloves to be precise, and first team hooker for the rugby fifteen which was my passion.

I remember one morning after playing cricket the evening prior I was confronted by one of the PE teachers who was known for his sergeant major like character, he shouted my name as he approached me on a stairwell. He pushed my face into the wall and put pressure on my jaw, which hurt. He was ranting and raving in a loud angry voice in front of a staircase full of other pupils, about how he had read the score book from the game last night and how disappointed he was at the amount of extras given away and blamed me and my inadequacy as the reason. I felt embarrassed, humiliated, frightened and angry with his actions, and didn't really know how to deal with the situation other than apologise through my teeth forced together by his fist on my jaw. The travesty of it all was revealed when I saw the score book after this unsavoury outburst. I had only let two byes go past. The other 20 or so extras were due to no balls, wides and leg byes, meaning the vast majority were certainly not down to my inability.

We had a French teacher called Mr Lewis who was not far off retirement and was a typical grammar school master. I disliked French immensely; I couldn't understand it. Ha, it was all French to me! Mr Lewis would stand in front of the class wearing his lecturer's gown and list on the blackboard past tense, present tense and past participles of the language. I didn't even know or understand what these points of grammar are in my own language never mind French. It soon became apparent that when Mr Lewis walked into the classroom shouting 'Bonjour la classe' as we were responding with 'Bonjour Monsieur Lewis' he would commence a search for a board rubber. If there wasn't one, he would leave us for five to ten minutes while he returned to the staffroom to find one.

This ritual led to us having a great idea – me and a fellow pupil, who was one of the year's bullies, came up with the concept, if we got rid of any board rubber before Mr Lewis entered the classroom the lesson would be cut short by five to ten minutes. Well, the class thought this was brilliant, so egged on by the majority each occasion we arrived in the classroom for French, any board rubber found would be despatched out of the window down into a culvert in the basement where the music department was situated. Result: each lesson was shortened while Mr Lewis set off to hunt down a substitute eraser. This was perceived a success for a short period while it created great hilarity among our peers, until the procedure ended abruptly!

Our form teacher of class 3T was a nice lady called Miss Foster who was a relatively new music teacher. One afternoon we all reported for registration to discover a pile of filthy, mouldy and damp board rubbers piled up on Miss Foster's desk – there must have been a dozen plus. At this point the big mistake happened. My partner in crime enquired:

"Where have those board rubbers come from?"

"The culvert outside the music room windows," she replied

"Oh! They must be the ones Carter and I threw out of French."

Mistake! Big mistake! Miss Foster was relatively calm but obviously annoyed. She had been down the culvert in wet, slimy and smelly conditions, collecting the discarded rubbers and was not best pleased. She cancelled her teaching me to play the kettle drums which I had started the previous week and that was what we thought was to be my only punishment. Oh no, how wrong could I be?

A few days later when the dust had settled and the incident forgotten about, or so we thought, we were in the middle of a biology lesson with Dr Burn when Mr Ford, head of French, knocked on the door and came in with a piece of paper in his hand.

"Sorry to interrupt, Dr Burn, but can I speak with these two boys outside please?"

Reading the piece of paper, Dr Burn looked up and pointing to me and my accomplice said, "You two, go with Mr Ford."

Clueless as to why he wanted to speak to us, we went outside the classroom. Mr Ford was very calm in manner and spoke to us in a quiet controlled voice. He asked the question:

"I understand you two are responsible for board rubbers being thrown out of the French classroom window?"

Now realising why we had been asked outside, we both shuffled and fidgeted nervously but in silence. Then with the loudest booming voice which must have shaken the hundred-year-old school and could have been heard in Leeds, he shouted,

"WELL!! ARE YOU?"

We both jumped out of our skins with the sudden sharp rise in volume. Our heads bowed and slouched even more with a silence of fear, and we sheepishly said, "Yes, Sir".

"Right, come and see me after school tomorrow and tell your parents you will be late home. Get back into class and apologise to Dr Burn for disturbing his lesson."

The following day, parents informed, school day completed and after a lot of discussion and apprehension about the punishment which was to confront us, after school we met Mr Ford, and he informed us what was in store. We would start in classroom one out of 52 and when we arrived at a classroom with no board rubber, we would go into classroom ten, stay there for an hour then come back the following day and start the process again. This would go on every night until every one of the 52 classrooms possessed a board rubber. So off we were marched escorted by Mr Ford to classroom one where we found a rubber then on to two, oops no board rubber here.

"OK, boys, off to classroom ten, do some homework or something, I'll be back in an hour."

So, there you have it: every night for the foreseeable future we were doomed unless there was a board rubber in all 52 classrooms.

Enter the intuition of a pair of schoolboys. The prospect of staying back indefinitely was not an option, so we spent all the next day, in between lessons, going round all the classrooms hunting for spare board rubbers. We checked most of the 52; if any classroom had more than one eraser, we took the surplus and stored them in our bags. We met up with Mr Ford at the end of the school day and off we went to classroom one, two, three, and four, etc. When we got to a classroom with no eraser, we would conveniently find one from within our bags. Eventually we arrived at classroom 52 and were satisfied there was an eraser in each room.

"Right then! You don't get away with it that easily, now go back to classroom one and clean every blackboard. When every board in the school is clean report to me in the main hall," Mr Ford instructed. So, the mission began, and to be fair a lot of the boards were clean, but quite a number did need a going over; if we found more erasers, we once again collected them in my bag. On completion of this strangely enjoyable marathon clean, we walked into the main hall to find Mr Ford on stage with the full cast of that year's school production.

We were covered from head to foot in chalk dust, our dark blue uniform enhancing the white powder, looking like we'd had a fight in a flour mill. The whole cast stopped singing intermittently as we strolled into the hall, they were wide eyed with jaws dropped as these two 'Pilsbury Dough boys' approached the stage. When Mr Ford saw us, he raised his hand to stop the chorus singing officially. Of course, at this point we were unaware of our white dusty appearance. He asked us, as he fought to hold back a chuckle:

"Have you completed the task?"

"Yes, Sir!" we replied in unison.

"Right then off you go and make sure you have learned your lesson."

"Yes, Sir!" we repeated, then I spoke up.

"Sir, just one thing, we have found a few extra board rubbers; what do you want us to do with them?"

"Put them on the piano in front of you, I'll sort them out later."

I think Mr Ford assumed there may be one or two, even half a dozen at most, but he had underestimated us as we piled well over 20 board rubbers on the mentioned piano. The full stage watched us gobsmacked and aghast, and Mr Williamson, the head of music, who had been playing the piano as we walked in had a look of total shock and horror on his face as more and more erasers were piled up on the school's prized and highly polished grand piano. We found the whole situation rather amusing as we exited the hall wearing large Cheshire Cat grins.

This whole exercise was by far the best detention I ever received in five years' attendance at Pudsey Grammar School. Lesson learnt, I have never ejected a board rubber out of a window since.

RUGBY THE EARLY DAYS

My interest in rugby all started as a 12-year-old when I was desperate to go watch live sport. On Sunday dinner times friends of Mum and Dad would occasionally call in with their son on the way to Odsal Stadium to watch Bradford Northern play rugby league. Three years earlier I had been taken to Headingley on my ninth birthday to see the Rugby League World Cup final between Great Britain and Australia, so I had been given a taste of the game. On one of the aforementioned Sundays I, as a cheeky pre-teenager, asked if I could come to the match with the three of them.

"Don't be cheeky," said Mum. "No, you can't," to which the two friends answered:

"Yes, he can if he wants," and so, after a bit of pleading with Mum I was allowed to attend.

Bradford Northern had been relegated to the second division at the end of the previous season and consequently were a bit too good for this standard. The previous week they had beaten Doncaster 73-3, were unbeaten and stood at the top of the second tier. On this day, the first day of my love of rugby, they were playing Huyton, a place I had never heard of and was told when I enquired, it was near Liverpool on Merseyside. I loved it! The atmosphere, the whole occasion, the colours, the noise and most of all the game, it was fantastic, I was in awe and wide eyed all afternoon. I just wanted more of this high and buzz. As our friends dropped me off at home the request was, can I come again? We'll see, came the uncommitted answer.

I had caught the bug, rugby was my passion, all the way through the 1970s I ate, slept and drank Bradford Northern, being picked up on a Sunday dinner time became the norm. I was taken to every home game, using my £1 annual schoolboy pass and most away games. By the end of the decade, I had attended every rugby league ground in the country. My school exercise books were covered with Bradford Northern slogans and crowd scenes drawn as I got bored in lessons. Dad frequently remarked if I'd 'spent as much time on my studies' as I did write 'Bradford Northern' on my books, I would 'have left school a genius'. I lived from week to week, Sunday was the focus, the main reason for living, it was all I thought about.

While all this was happening in the mid 70s I was a pupil attending Pudsey Grammar School when me and two fellow pupils noticed a windscreen sticker on a side window of the school minibus. This sticker was advertising the fact Bingley Rugby Union Club wanted under 19s to join their expanding Colts section. We were all three interested and after a bit of simple detective work found out the sticker was put there by one of the geography teachers who played in the Bingley first fifteen on a weekend. We expressed an interest and was told to attend the ground at Wagon Lane, Bingley at a particular date and time so we could join the Colts. The Colts played every Sunday morning which clashed with Sunday School. I dreaded telling Mum and Dad I wanted to exchange church for the rugby field, but when I announced my decision surprisingly there was very little resistance. So, on a Sunday we would walk the mile to Thornbury, catch the bus to Bingley, play rugby, home and away, bus back to Thornbury, walk the mile home, arriving just in time to be taken to Odsal to watch my beloved Bradford Northern.

This routine became the norm every Sunday, the three of us on the upstairs of one of Bradford's finest buses watching the world pass on our way to play. Then repeat homeward carrying black eyes, swollen lips, blooded noses, knocks, bruises and other battle scars. I suspect we looked a right bonny bunch, and I adored it. I loved the camaraderie, the physicality, and the intensity of the game as much as I cherished watching Bradford Northern, although playing was in my mind far better than spectating. My position was hooker, the mad man in the middle of the front row. I was made for that position, small, fat (with weight) but very supple and flexible due to my gymnastics background, which enabled me to operate very low in the scrum. I embraced running with the ball, tackling (my favourite), rucking, mauling, scrummaging and throwing the ball into the line out. Rarely was I a violent player, my philosophy in the scrum was 'it's up to you, mate'. I wanted to play hard and fair but if my opposite number wanted to carry out unsportsmanlike scrum antics, I would meet them with great resolve and often finish it. It was always their choice as to whether we went down that route or not.

One of my less fine moments on the rugby field during this period was when we played Ilkley Colts. They had a scrum half called Nigel Melville, yes, the same who became England captain. He was outstanding then even at that early age, and it was obvious he could go far. My coach had instructed me that when Ilkley had a line out and won the ball, I was to get round the front and tackle the scrum half to stop him offloading the ball or at least make him conscious of my presence. The whole of the first half I tried my damnedest to get hold of Melville but realistically he was just too good and quick. I never got to lay a finger on him, the ball was away in the blink of an eye. At half time the coach got into my ribs about making their scrum half know I was there; he suggested all sorts of ways I could do it. But I don't think he intended for me to do what I did. First line out of the second half Ilkley won the ball, Melville received it and sent it down the line, four seconds later... BANG!! I hit him from behind round the jaw. From the moment I connected I knew I was wrong; I didn't cause a lot of injury, but he knew I was there, this was not the way I wanted to play this great game. By today's standards I would definitely be sent off! There was no subtlety in my actions; it was a piece of downright thuggery. They got the penalty and took it as Melville was being treated and helped to his feet. I felt so guilty, rather than slowing him down, the event slowed me down as I didn't particularly want to get near him for the rest of the game. A lesson learnt for me, I did get praise from my coach and teammates for my action, but it felt wrong to me and something I'm not proud of.

The following season I was picked to attend trials for the Yorkshire Colts taking place in York. My coach at Bingley said there was no point in me catching a bus from Thornbury to Bingley for me to get in a car and be driven to York back via Leeds. He rung me a few evenings before the actual date to inform me he had arranged for the Colts coach at Phoenix Park Rugby Club to pick me up outside the Territorial Army Barracks on Bradford Road at a specific time. So that Saturday morning a white car driven by a total stranger picked me up and took me to York. As I sat in the front seat three unknown Phoenix Park Colts were squeezed in the rear seats, all who in later years became very good friends; the coach spent the whole of the journey asking me why I didn't play for Phoenix Park, blatant poaching!

"So, let me get this straight, every Sunday morning you walk up to Thornbury, pass Phoenix Park, to catch a bus to go play rugby at Bingley?" he queried.

"Yes, that's right," I answered nervously.

"Well, why don't you just walk to Thornbury and play rugby for us? It will save you a bus ride, no bus fare and you won't have to get up as early, would you?"

"No," I said.

Of course, everything he said made total sense, for a 17-year-old, especially the bit about not getting up as early.

We arrived at the ground and were shown to the changing rooms, dressed into our rugby kit, and split into teams. We were briefed about the structure of the day, how it would work and told there would be coaches in the stands scrutinising each player in every different position. My problem was, because the distance and travel time to Bingley was so far, I couldn't afford the time or bus fare to train twice a week, and I was never the best motivated trainer, so I only played. This alluded to me not being fit enough for the Yorkshire Colts, although I knew inside, I was good enough. In the second short trial game I played, I was in a scrum, against an opposition far stronger, they drove through our scrum, my arm got trapped and my shoulder was slowly eased out of its socket and dislocated. The pain was excruciating and yes, I did scream. As the scrum broke, I was left holding my right arm, experiencing massive discomfort and agony. Medics rushed onto the field of play, saw the state of my misshaped shoulder and summoned an ambulance.

The trip in the ambulance from York Rowntree's rugby pitches to The York Hospital was not too far but my shoulder felt every crack, pothole and undulation in the York roads. I was wheeled into casualty and straight into a cubicle where a doctor and nurse managed with great care to remove my soiled rugby shirt and then what seemed to be all in one motion relocated my shoulder back into its natural position. The pain again was agonising, but the medical professionals managed to do it swiftly. I was then informed all I needed was an X-ray to ensure there was no structural damage.

"Oh no! That's going to take hours," I stated.

"It shouldn't, you're next on the list," replied the nurse.

So off I was wheeled to the X-ray department to get my shoulder seen to.

Unbeknown to me, while I was in X-ray two emergency cases were being admitted into the hospital, one was a child who had fallen out of a tree, and I am unsure what the other involved. This all led to the few medical staff on duty that Saturday afternoon being relocated to deal with these two very urgent cases, meaning I was left in my cubicle dressed topless in muddy rugby shorts, socks and boots for four more hours.

As I sat there in my half-nakedness, waiting, waiting and waiting, bored, with thoughts running through my head it suddenly dawned on me 'how was I going to get home?' – the rugby trials would've finished hours ago, nobody had escorted me in the ambulance, I hadn't seen the Phoenix Park coach since he'd left the four of us at the changing rooms and I didn't believe my Bingley coach was even in attendance. So, what am I to do? Should I get the bus, or the train supporting a knackered shoulder dressed only in dirty rugby kit? I was at a loss, as these ideas were bouncing round my mind, I was informed a Yorkshire Colts official was waiting for me in the casualty reception. Another gentleman I had never met and didn't know was there waiting to take me home. So much for not getting into cars with strangers, I'd done it twice in one day. He was a very nice man who had retrieved my bag and belongings from the changing rooms and followed the ambulance to the hospital. I felt very guilty and sorry for him, I'm sure he could have done several things more constructive that afternoon than wait for me for four hours. An hour and a half or so after my X-rays were finished a nurse came into the cubicle and clipped the photographs onto a light box. I was so bored I examined this piece of evidence and with the voice of a medical expert said to the nurse:

"I've looked at the X-rays and I can't see any sign of structural damage so could you put them in an envelope and send me to my local hospital where I can make an outpatient appointment for further treatment?"

"No, I can't do that, it has to be seen by a doctor to make an official diagnosis, I'm sorry," she said with sympathy. Consequently, after four hours sat in the cubicle, a doctor appeared, glanced at the X-rays and spoke.

"That's good! There is no structural damage," he said, turning to the nurse. "Put the slides in an envelope and send him home to his local hospital to make an outpatients appointment." Brilliant, I thought, I could have done that two and a half hours earlier.

X-rays completed and put in an envelope, showing no signs of structural damage just assumed ligament issues, I was dressed in a sling and sent home with letters and paperwork instructing me to attend Leeds General Infirmary outpatients who would advise me on further treatment and recouperation. I was off work approximately six weeks and given exercises and physiotherapy to aid my recovery. With all this downtime I got thinking about what the Phoenix Park coach had said about walking up to their rugby club to catch a bus, sit on it for 40 minutes, to get to my rugby club to play a game of Colts' rugby. When I regained my fitness, I decided it would be beneficial to join Phoenix Park which was approximately 11 miles nearer home, bit of a no brainer really. I phoned the coach at Bingley which took a bit of courage as I thought I was letting him down, but he took the news quite sympathetically and understood my reasons for changing clubs. From that moment Phoenix Park became my rugby club.

On one Sunday morning Phoenix Park Colts were playing Roundhay Colts. Prior to this fixture it became apparent there were too many 'Andys' in the team, every time the coaches called out 'Andy' four of us would stop to discover it was one of the other three the coach was referring to. It became obvious nicknames would have to be decided upon, but what? Andy 1,2,3 and 4 were not an option, also Andy followed by our surname, initial was not acceptable, so the challenge was on. During this game against Roundhay they had a rather large number eight, over six foot tall as an under-19, and anyone who knows me realises I lack inches in height. This number eight punched me in a maul and as we broke away, I swung a fist in his direction. Five foot some verses six-foot plus was always going to be a mismatch to say the least. My swing missed by miles as all the onlookers thought this sight was one of the funniest things they'd seen on a rugby field. Then one smart aleck recounting the incident in the clubhouse bar after the game with great mirth compared me to the character 'Lofty' in the 70s sitcom 'It 'aint half hot mum' and it stuck. Ever since then in rugby circles, I am known as LOFTY!

I played Colts rugby on Sunday mornings and was soon drafted to play senior rugby for the thirds, seconds and occasionally the first team on Saturdays. Two games a weekend, what would the authorities say about that these days? I learned a lot about the game from the older experienced senior players and my thirst for learning held no boundaries. On one occasion I was playing for the third team against Hullencians, and their tight head prop was really getting under my skin using all sorts of front row shenanigans, we were having a right tussle. My second rower, a guy who played over five hundred games for the club, realised my plight and pulled me over to one side. He said,

"Lofty, don't get involved, just do your job, rely on your talent and all will end well. I've played against him for years and know what he's like, just don't be drawn in and react, that's what he wants."

Wise words indeed, we packed down at the next scrum and the prop dropped his head so low I couldn't see the ball entering the scrum for me to hook. The scrum half and I used the tap method which meant when I was ready for the ball I'd tap my hand, when he saw this signal, he would put the ball in the scrum, and I'd hook it. This procedure was carried out to perfection, and I hooked the ball, as the scrum broke apart, I happened to mention to the prop with some authority,

"See! I can even do it with my eyes shut!"

Well, he didn't seem to like the fact I'd got one over him, so he reacted with venom and threw a punch which glanced off my forehead. Unfortunately for him this was right in front of the referee's nose who promptly sent him off as me and my second rower chuckled with glee. That's an example of the voice of experience.

I loved playing for Phoenix Park, I also loved watching Bradford Northern. I am not of the opinion rugby union is better than rugby league or in fact vice versa. In my eyes they are two totally different games which can be enjoyed by all, they use a similar pitch, same shaped ball and posts, but this is where the similarities end. I have found it is usually rugby league fans who tell me their code is better than union, it's like they must justify their preference and have an inferiority complex or chip on their shoulder. Enjoy both! And if you can't, why criticize the other completely different, fantastic game!

COLLEGE

I was not the best of scholars at school, when I left Pudsey Grammar School in 1978, I was armed with one 'O' level which was English. ENGLISH?! I hear you cry, what with the spelling and grammar in these stories I know it will come as a bit of a surprise, I have said on numerous occasions I suspect the examination board felt sorry for me and awarded me English 'O' level out of sympathy. So, on leaving school what to do? I found myself enrolling at Airedale and Wharfedale College of Further Education to retake my failed 'O' levels in Maths, Physics, Biology and Chemistry.

Airedale and Wharfedale gave me an education, but certainly not an academic one. My first disappointment with the college was that on a Wednesday afternoon most further education establishments kept the timetable free for students to pursue sporting activities, huh! When I attended the college, it was explained to me that they had messed up the timetable, and me and some fellow classmates would have to spend Wednesday afternoons attending triple chemistry located in a temporary classroom overlooking the rugby pitch. This was hardly conducive to chemistry motivation, particularly when it was a subject I found difficult, taught by a part-time lecturer who came across as someone who would much prefer to be elsewhere. I can't remember her name, but she was a large rotund woman who in my opinion was just stealing a salary. She appeared to know her subject, but her teaching skills were non-existent. Add all this to my lack of interest, understanding and motivation in the subject, my mates playing rugby, my passion, out on the field within my eyeline, meant that the small flames of interest I had for chemistry were quickly extinguished. This is by no means an excuse, more a list of facts. I am not blaming anybody but myself for my failure in this subject, as I am a firm believer in taking responsibility for your own actions and in this case my actions were by no means exemplary.

The other subjects I did at college weren't any better, but at least I had some sort of understanding of them, although again outside influences were a big distraction. It was the year 1978/79, and I discovered smoking, alcohol and girls. Up to this point in my life I was a staunch anti-smoker. I don't know why I started smoking, perhaps it was peer pressure, but then again not many in my close friendship group smoked. I remember being offered a cigarette by a fellow student and after a few puffs I felt nauseous, headachy and dizzy, it wasn't a pleasant feeling at all. This should have been a good enough reason for me never to pick up a cigarette again, I even skulked to the toilets to save face and discard the offending stick of tobacco. This awful experience was soon forgotten, though, and I had battled through the symptoms and then had another until soon I was buying packets of 20 cigarettes. At the time in typical Andy Carter fashion, I enjoyed one of the most expensive brands of cigarettes on the market, which obviously cost more of the very little money I had at the time. I developed a smoker's cough and was bringing up dark grey phlegm in a morning around the time I met Julie in June 1985. For this reason – Julie's insistence and support and my own willpower – I had my last cigarette on 31st August 1985. Roll on to December 1985 while on the Scouts Christmas camp of that year, we had all eaten a large Christmas dinner and I craved for a smoke, none of the other leaders, all who smoked, would give me a cigarette, saying,

"No chance, you've stopped."

So off I went into the kitchen with a bit of a huff and a sulk to start the mammoth task of washing up. On the kitchen windowsill I spied an open packet of Silk Cut cigarettes. I was desperate, I needed the fix even though I'd given up three and a half months earlier. So, I pinched one. Wrong move! It was a big disappointment – it didn't taste or feel as I remembered and after four of five puffs it started, the nausea, headache and slight dizziness. I couldn't get rid of it quick enough. I disposed of the offending article as quick as possible and continued with the washing up duties, never to have a cigarette touch my lips again.

The first day we started at Airedale and Wharfedale College was the day I discovered alcohol. We were 16, and I am not saying I had never been in a pub before, but it was the start of me attending pubs on a regular basis. Unlike today, I was never questioned about my age or asked for proof or ID. We went to college on that first day to complete registration protocol and administration, then found ourselves at a loose end by dinner time, so along with my best friend at the time we headed out of the college grounds and straight into The Fleece public house on New Road Side in Horsforth. We ordered a pint and a sandwich. I don't know whether they knew we were underage or not, or if they just turned a blind eye, but we got served with no questions asked. I believe in those days, like the drink driving laws, these rules were not as strictly adhered to as they are today. It was soon decided that The Fleece was a bit too posh for us, so we wandered that little bit further to The Stanhope which is now known as the Eleventh Earl. The Stanhope was a Bass pub which served Stones Bitter, but my favourite drink was a pint of Blue, which was a mild. We frequented this pub so often by the time we left college I had got to know all the bar staff and when I walked in to be asked, "Is it the usual, Andy?" in my mind it meant I had arrived. I believed it was a bit of a badge of honour.

If we weren't in lectures or The Stanhope, we spent a lot of down time in the students' common room. This was the hub of the college; this is where friendships were made and galvanised. It was a place where extra-curricular arrangement would be made, activities such as nightclubbing – at 17? – cinema, ice-skating, nights out and the odd house party were all planned. There was a canteen where I discovered pie, chips, gravy and coleslaw. Don't knock it till you try it. I ate this for my dinner every time I dined in the canteen. It was an issue if I got to the coleslaw bowl at the end of the line and it had all gone. In the common room area was a juke box which was played constantly, it had all the hits of the day on it as well as 60s and 70s classics. Along with the vibrant hum of students, chatting, laughing and smoking, it all maintained a very happy atmosphere.

Looking back, College was a year of adolescent fun, immature fun, it was the first time we were out of school and not told what to do and what not to do. We were expected to be responsible and act accordingly. We were given freedom, required to attend lectures but were never questioned if we missed any. We discovered life, we were trusted to get there and return home each day. The friendships we made would last forever or so we thought, it was a time in our lives where everything mattered, even the simple, unimportant things. It was the time 1978 to 1979 when I emerged from being an immature teenager into an immature adult. As friends we were tight as a drum, it was a fledgling year where we were released into the great wide world to start standing on our own two feet. It was that strange time in most people's lives when we thought we were no longer children, but the rest of the population didn't quite consider us adult yet!

GRANDPARENTS

Over my lifetime I have had five grandparents with each of whom I had a different relationship. Grandad Alf died before I was born, he was involved in a motorcycle accident in 1958. Grandad Carter I never knew as a well man, having had a stroke the year I was born, and died in 1976 aged 84. Grandma Carter died in 1982 aged 84, she is the one grandparent I have most guilt about, which I will explain. Grandma May (Granny May) was the grandparent I knew the longest, she died in 1999 aged 93 and her second husband Grandad Arthur, who I never really had a relationship with, died on a London Underground platform of a heart attack, I don't know which year this was.

Every other Sunday through my childhood, Dad, Mum, Elaine and I would go to Grandma Carter's for a Sunday salad tea. Uncle Leslie (Dad's brother) and his wife Aunty Grace would also attend with my cousins Antonia, Peter and Jill, who were all a few years older than me. Aunty Marjorie (Dad's sister) would also be there unless she was working as a Sister at The Women's Hospital in Leeds. These Sundays to a child were the most boring of days, it seemed the world would stop, all the men and children would be banished to the front living room where they would sit in silence and stare at the four walls with the odd observational comment, debate and chitter chatter were not commonplace. There was a clock on the mantlepiece which would tick, tick and tick, louder and louder and louder as the silence became more deafening. No television was allowed, not on a Sunday, no playing the upright organ, which was stood against the wall in the room, basically because no one other than Uncle Leslie could get a tune out of it. So, if on the rare occasion Elaine and I were allowed to have a go, the noise came out as musical drivel which was soon stopped, and silence and the ticking would return.

Tick, tick, tick as the clock went on, the sound being the only noise within the room, seemingly getting louder with each second. Elaine and I may be doing some drawing, colouring or playing a simple quiet game, but it was a case of amuse yourselves as the adults were not interested; these were the days when children were to be seen and not heard, it amuses me to think how this oppression would be viewed these days. Tick, tick, tick the clock moved slowly on. Occasionally my cousin Peter, who was one of my childhood heroes, would take me for a walk down to the local mill dam to observe the swans. These rare outings provided a welcome distraction from the monotony and incessant ticking of the clock, tick, tick, tick, on and on it went.

Eventually one of the ladies would appear from the dining room to assemble a round card table, and dress it with a tablecloth – this was the signal that tea was imminent. All the men would then be ushered through to the dining room as Grandad Carter would be abandoned to eat his tea on his own in the lounge with only the ticking of the clock as company, tick, tick, tick. I don't understand to this day why food was transported from the dining room into the lounge for Grandad Carter to sit and eat his tea in isolation. He'd had a stroke in 1961, the year I was born – perhaps this had something to do with the reason, but other than repeating himself Elaine and I never detected a problem. This was the common practice and ritual every other Sunday for many years, it would end with Uncle Leslie and family leaving not long after we had eaten to go and attend the evening service at their church. We would wave them off as they drove up the street in their family's white mark 2 Jaguar.

When Grandma Carter passed away, I did have a sense of guilt, this might have been due to these routine and uninspired Sundays spent at her house. As I grew into my teens, I should have known better and realised she was not responsible for the mundane visits, but still immaturely I would often resist any invite to go and see her. She had lived with Aunty Marjorie since Grandad Carter's passing, but when Aunty Marjorie was on nights at the hospital, she would spend time between her shifts living in the nurses' home which meant Grandma Carter was to all intents and purposes living on her own. One day shortly before she died, I declined the chance to go visit her, I got my way, but Dad happened to mention that Grandma Carter loved me very much and really looked forward to and enjoyed the times I visited. To be fair, when I did make the effort or couldn't get out of visiting, I always came home armed with some chocolate or other treats, and the visits, other than the regular childhood Sundays, could be quite inspiring, but the memories and boredom of those tick ticking Sundays were deeply branded within my brain. I didn't go see her that day and never got a chance to see her again. Another classic case of wishing I knew what I know now…then! I did attend

Grandma Carter's funeral, I was 20 years old, and I shed tears of grief and guilt, due to not seeing her more when given the chance. I remember Peter had made the journey from South Wales to attend the funeral and after the bun fight at Norwood Avenue, Dad's childhood home, he had to leave early for the long drive back. As he was leaving and saying his goodbyes, he mentioned to Aunty Marjorie he was pleased he could make it, to which, quite curtly she told him he shouldn't be pleased to attend any funeral no matter whose it is, which is not I suspect exactly what he meant.

Granny May was my closest grandparent, how the times had changed – she would come to our house every other Sunday for dinner with Aunty Marjorie, they both by now lived in Pudsey. As I remember we didn't have a ticking clock and due to Elaine and I being much older, we were allowed to do our own thing, come and go as we pleased as long as we were at the table when dinner was served or given enough notice when we wouldn't be attending. Often this would be in the form of a typical Sunday roast prepared by Dad, rather than the salad tea of years earlier. Bless her, as Granny May got older, she would fall asleep in the chair, with her chin on her chest with her dentures falling out, it did make us smile. One of my earliest memories of Granny May was going to see her in a little back-to-back house in Milford Place in Heaton. I also remember her coming swimming with us at Aireborough Swimming Baths wearing a vivid red swimsuit. It just shows how time passes on, I guess when Granny May was in that red swimming costume, she would have been a similar age to what I am now, perhaps even a couple of years younger.

Granny May had two husbands in her life, Grandad Alf who was Mum's biological farther, he died in 1958, three years before I was born. From the stories I have been told he was riding pillion on a motor scooter when it was involved in a road accident. He died from his injuries in hospital a few days later. Granny May once told me she wondered if she had been part of his demise because when she went to see him all he wanted was a bottle of Brown Ale, but the hospital nursing staff would not allow it, in fact they forbid it. The following visit she smuggled in a couple of bottles which he consumed with great enjoyment and delight. The following day he passed away. I did assure her this, in my opinion, would not have accelerated his demise and I think she knew this and told the tale with tongue in cheek; we got solace from believing he died a happy man having had the opportunity to enjoy two bottles of his favourite ale. I told the story of Grandad Alf's death to Julie's family while sat round the table one mealtime, it turns out that Donald, Julie's dad, used to work with Grandad Alf at Carter Gears in Thornbury, Bradford and remembered the motorbike accident he was involved in. Donald spoke of Grandad Alf with the utmost respect and admiration of his mentor when Donald was a junior engineer… Small World!

Granny May's second husband was Grandad Arthur; she lived with him in a quadrangle of terraced cottages known as Lilycroft Tradesmen's Houses; they qualified to live there because Arthur was a retired greengrocer tradesman. He had a daughter called Francis who became Mum's stepsister. Arthur died suddenly on a platform on the London Underground while delivering Christmas presents to family he was visiting in London. I don't know who said it, but his death was described as 'he was dead before he hit the ground' caused due to a massive heart attack. This is possibly the way we would all want to go with no suffering and not knowing anything about it. The only downside I can see dying in this way is that it is such a massive shock for the loved ones left behind. No warning, no build up, just gone instantly, wow what a shock.

In conclusion I can say I never knew any of my grandparents particularly well and I think they all have a history I am not aware of. Granny May was the closest possibly because she lived the longest. Grandad Alf I never met but have heard lots about. Grandad Carter, I never knew as a well man, but as children he would entertain us in his own funny way, and Grandma Carter never received as much of my love and attention as she deserved due to my immature and self-centred teenage years. Grandad Arthur was just the guy who lived with Granny May. In short, I loved and admired each and every one of them and I am proud and honoured they each have played their part in mine and my family's history.

THE DEPARTMENT OF TEXTILE INDUSTRIES

16th July 1979 proved to be quite an important day in my life – it was the day I started work as a Junior Technician at Leeds University in the Textile Department. After leaving Airedale and Wharfedale College having sat my 'O' levels for the second time, the focus turned to finding a job or career for my life ahead. I was 17 and thought I was invincible, I had discovered smoking, drinking and girls at the college with not a care in the world, but now things were turning a bit more serious as my future became more significant.

In 1979 the job situation and prospects were not good, unemployment was high and the job market virtually non-existent. What could I do? I couldn't join the fire service as I was not yet 18 and getting a trade did not really appeal to me although I would have tried anything. So, with all this in mind it was arranged that not long after sitting my last 'O' level exam I would meet Dad, who at the time worked at the Leeds Polytechnic in the Art Education Department across the road from the Merrion Centre. Situated in the office block above the Merrion Centre was the Careers Advice Department. This was a place school leavers could go to find out what job opportunities were available. I met Dad, who had made the appointment, and we went to see what they had to offer. I had absolutely no idea whatsoever what I wanted to do or pursue as a career. Due to the subjects I had attempted at 'O' level, the obvious path would be one with a science influence. But I was at a complete loss as to what to do. I really wanted to join the fire service but I was too young and other than that the only other job I had ever expressed an interest in doing was to become a television cameraman, and that was only because I would be allowed to attend major sporting events for free, hardly a reason to base a career on. To say I was open minded and ready to take on anything suggested was a bit of an understatement.

As expected, because of my 'O' levels it was recommended I should find something in the field of science. Elida Gibb, Sandoz, Yorkshire Chemicals and one of the Leeds Teaching Hospitals all had vacancies for juniors. As we were on the verge of leaving the careers office armed full of job seekers advice with interviews to arrange, the lady I had seen pulled a card out of a file and reading it said:

"This came in this morning, Leeds University Textile Department are looking for a junior technician in their Dyeing, Finishing and Printing division, would that be of any interest?"

Interest? Of course I hadn't got a clue, textiles was an industry which had never crossed my mind, but hey ho let's give it a go, what had I to lose?

The visit to the Careers Advice office resulted in four interviews, the first was at a chemical company called Elida Gibb, then another pharmaceutical company called Sandoz based in Rodley, Leeds, a third in the pathology department at the Leeds General Infirmary and of course the late addition at Leeds University Textile Department. The first two were particularly uninspiring, and not really for me, which is rich coming from someone who didn't really know what he wanted to do anyway, and could I afford to be picky in such a sparce job market? The third was quite interesting but seemed to involve a lot of mundane tasks. The one that interested me most was the Leeds University job; I applied and got an interview and was quite hopeful of success. I presented myself at the Man-made Fibres Building of the Textile Department at my allotted time, it was a large four-storey 1960s concrete and brick building, with large wide, white stone steps leading up to a huge oak double door. Once inside there was a double staircase leading up the floors and a small reception area behind glass where I had been instructed to wait.

Another male candidate was sat in the reception area who asked me if I was there for the interview. I confirmed I was and soon realised that this guy was my opposition, well for that day at least. After a short time, we were confronted by two elderly gentlemen. One was wearing a white lab coat covered in a multitude of colours, Mr Jack Jones, and the other was a short more important looking man dressed in a three-piece suit with a pair of glasses on a chain round his neck; he introduced himself as Dr Bell, the academic responsible for the dyeing, finishing and printing area within the whole textile department. It was decided that Jack would show me round the sheds and machinery, which was basically the whole ground floor of the Man-made Fibres building, while the other candidate would go to Dr Bell's office to discuss the job role, job description, pay, grade, qualifications, hours and expected responsibilities.

Then after about forty minutes we would swap over. I really enjoyed the trip round the machines of the department, Stenter, Jigger, Autoclave, Winch and Calendar, not that I had any understanding of these machines' capabilities and uses, even though Jack tried his best to explain. What I did find exciting was the print room which had neoprene covered tables ten metres long with printed fabric stuck to them. I thought I would enjoy working here and the explained procedure seemed straightforward.

After about forty minutes to an hour, we met up with Dr Bell and the other candidate to swap roles. I went upstairs with Dr Bell to his office on the second floor while the other chap left with jack to do the tour I had just completed. Dr Bell explained what would be expected of me, he explained the pay, holiday entitlement and that if successful I would be on a junior Technicians grade. Then he got to the nitty gritty, my pending 'O' level results and asked how I thought I had done. Genuinely I was sure I'd done particularly well, and I managed to convince the academic of my confidence. So much so he said that even if I'd had a disaster, I would have got at least two. The interviews with Jack and Dr Bell went well and I liked what I'd seen and been told. On my way out of the building I bumped into the other guy who told me he wasn't interested and had told them so. Well at least that's one less candidate which made my odds of getting the job slightly better.

Later that day I got a phone call from Dr Bell informing me I had been successful and he would like to offer me the position of Junior technician in the Dyeing, Finishing and Printing in the Textile Department at Leeds University. Of course, I was delighted to accept the offer and confirmed I could start on Monday 16th of July 1979. That was that: I started work on that day and I loved it, especially the printing. My fellow colleagues were lovely, my working conditions and environment were idyllic, and my immediate boss, Jack, was tremendous, although his first words to me were:

"Good morning, Andy, how old are you again?"

"Seventeen," I replied.

"Seventeen, eh, well I've got eight years to do then I'm off!"

What he meant was he was winding down for retirement as he'd had enough. All was going swimmingly until the third Thursday in August to be precise. I awoke that morning and was lying in my bed when my mother opened the door and threw an envelope in my direction, then left shutting the door with force. I don't know to this day what prompted this action, but this is what she did – perhaps she had some prior knowledge of the contents within the letter.

The envelope contained my 'O' level results. I opened it with eagerness, convinced it would be good news reading four passes…it didn't…four fails! My heart sank, my mood plummeted, as I read them again, just in case I had misunderstood them. I stared at them willing them to miraculously change in front of my eyes…no, they didn't. When Mum asked about them, she reacted with a shrug which basically meant she wasn't surprised. Huh! So much for the vote of confidence and the rallying of positive comments. I was responsible for the failure; I was reaping the reward for spending more time in The Stanhope than in class at Airedale and Wharfedale College. Crushed and gutted were two of the many emotions I experienced that morning, but they were nothing compared to the feeling of trepidation, anxiety and fear as it slowly dawned on me that I had to go to work that morning and inform Dr Bell I had failed all four exams, the same ones I had convinced him six week earlier I had done really well in.

The journey to work that morning was subdued to say the least, Dad was driving and not a lot was said. All I could think of was what would Dr Bell say? What would Jack's reaction be? And would I still have a job at the end of the day? Would it be a case of going to work with a job in the morning and returning home without a job in the evening… oh the dread!! I walked into work in a bit of a daze and anxiety about me. The first person I told about my failings was Jack, who to be fair commiserated with me but didn't appear or react too concerned. He did say I would have to go see Dr Bell who didn't usually arrive till after 0930hrs. Oh no! Another forty minutes of torture to endure!

I knew Dr Bell's routine and watched him as he walked across the car park and into the building. I heard him down the corridor, climb the two flights of stairs to his office. Still keeping out of sight I heard his office door unlocking and opening as he was unaware of the pending confrontation with a very timid, nervous Junior Technician about to knock on his door. I waited ten minutes or so before I knocked, I heard the command 'Enter' and walked into his office.

It didn't take me long to embarrassingly and ashamedly deliver the news. Dr Bell was obviously not best pleased but like Jack he was very calm and particularly non-plussed about the situation. Perhaps I wasn't going to be sacked after all. He explained that the reason I required the 'O' levels was to get me onto the day release course I was to be sent on at Bradford College. Bizarre, I know, being sent from a university to a college for further education. Dr Bell suggested I went to see Les Brayshaw who was the education officer for all the technical staff. Les was the academic-related technician in the warping and weaving department. Les's office was like a small internal hut located in the corner of the weaving shed. I told Les the problem, so he sat me down, got out a large pile of papers from a filing cabinet. After a short chat and a quick read of the papers over a cup of coffee he suggested I left it with him. Yet again I had to wait some time to learn of my pending fate, but on the positive side the powers that be – Dr Bell, Jack and Les – all seemed calm, matter of fact and generally unconcerned about my plight. Eventually, after what seemed an eternity, Les rung me to inform me, I could do a foundation course before I started the BTec Course in Textile Colouration.

Yes!! Yes!! Yes!! The relief was unbelievable. I was saved; well, my job was. I would be coming to work tomorrow after all. Fantastic! Life and my future were suddenly looking very bright!

SCARRED FOR LIFE

January 28th in 1981, was the day I was scarred for life! If anyone has been in the unfortunate position of seeing me without a shirt on, they will most certainly have noticed the 12-inch scar running vertically up the right-hand side of my abdomen. This is the lasting result of the day I had a cholecystectomy, or for the uneducated, my gallbladder removed. This was before laparoscopic cholecystectomy, keyhole surgery, was developed and long before lithotripsy was even thought about, which is the process of shattering gallstones with soundwaves.

It all started with a trip to the doctors, I had been suffering from abdominal pains on and off for some time. It was excruciating pain which would very slowly subside over a 36-hour period. We were patients at a surgery run by two brothers, Doctors Ian and James McTavish. These two doctors were chalk and cheese. James was a stylish slim gentleman who enjoyed marathon running, and portrayed an appearance of being a clean living and extremely fit individual. Ian was the complete opposite – when you entered his consultation room he would be sat at an old writing bureau with a glass of whisky and a cigar resting in an ashtray. His room would have a haze of smoke hanging below the ceiling as he looked at you over his half-moon spectacles, dressed in a three-piece tweed suit and speaking with a strong Sottish brogue. They were both lovely GPs, but Ian was my favourite.

It was Dr Ian, as he was known, who diagnosed the possibility of my problem being caused by gallstones. He referred me to the Leeds General Infirmary (LGI) for tests to confirm this. I was only 18 at the time and the so-called experts at the hospital refused to accept that a patient so young could be suffering with gallstones. But they did acknowledge I had an issue, so in their wisdom they decided to test me for everything except gallstones. They carried out more than one endoscopy in the search for ulcers, I had radioactive dye administered into my blood, which was quite unpleasant, to check my kidneys, and I had blood tests to confirm my problem wasn't appendix-related or other identifiable problems, followed by several other tests. Eventually after not finding a significant issue and at what appeared to be a resigned acceptance, it was decided to test me for gallstones. This test was ironically the simplest of them all – my stomach was swathed in gel and an ultrasound scanner was rubbed over me. This is the same test given to twelve-week pregnant ladies. Low and behold they found gallstones, some of which were blocking my bile duct which was the source of the pain. Alleluja!

I was admitted to hospital, now being 19, on Thursday 22nd January 1981. As I was preparing myself for the pending ordeal my mother pointed at my abdomen, commenting on how smooth it appeared and after today it would never look the same again. Cheers, Mother! This did absolutely nothing to ease my already shot mental anxiety, fear and nerves. We arrived at ward 27 ready to check in, I was shown to a bed in a bay of four and settled in. Blood pressure, pulse, temperature, blood and urine samples were taken, as I was left alone to get on with things, no holding hands or accompaniment in those days. The word had got round the Textile Department at Leeds University where I worked, that 'Andy had been admitted to hospital'. Consequently, that evening ward 27 was invaded by dozens of female textile designers all coming to visit me. This did not go down too well with the nursing staff and as the sergeant major type Staff Nurse Bright was passing my bed she sternly commented,

"You are only allowed two visitors per bed, not a dozen!"

My visitors took it upon themselves and dispersed to introduce themselves to other patients who did not have visitors that evening, taking turns to return to my bed two at a time. When visiting was over, signalled by a bell, I received many thanks from other patients on the ward for bringing the students in to visit. It went down a storm but I'm not sure Staff Nurse Bright saw the positive side.

The following morning, I was woken at 0600hrs by the voice of Staff Nurse Bright telling me to wake up. I opened my eyes to see her stood over me holding a glass of water above my head.

"You wouldn't," I said.

"She would!" said the three other patients in unison.

I followed their advice and didn't call her bluff, because in our fledgling relationship I realised pouring a glass of water over my head was not out of the realms of possibility. That morning, I was informed of some good news, I wasn't due to have my operation until sometime the following week so there was no point me staying in a hospital bed in a very well state for the weekend, so I had to promise more than once if they let me home I would be back first thing Monday morning. Of course I assured the medical staff I would return, so I was allowed home for a two-day break. This in principle was good for me but it just prolonged my worry and anxiety about the pending procedure.

The weekend went quite slowly; I tried to distract myself by keeping busy but there was a constant cloud at the back of my mind trying to anticipate the unknown. On the Friday night I went to a house party where I found myself sat with my own nervous thoughts while the rest of the guests mingled and moved around. People were interested in my upcoming surgery and assured me I would be fine, offering encouragement and sympathy. However, it was easy for them to make these reassuring comments, it wasn't happening to them, it was me who would have to deal with the experience. On the Sunday I went as usual to watch my beloved Bradford Northern, rugby league was my passion, the match did take my mind off things for a couple of hours but after the game the demons returned.

Monday morning saw me return to ward 27. Was my weekend away from the hospital any good? I don't know, perhaps it was better doing things rather than sat on a hospital bed twiddling my thumbs with thoughts churning, still not knowing when the operation would be performed. I was told on Tuesday morning it was to be carried out the following morning at 1000hrs. Wow! Now it seemed real. I watched the other guys in the bay go down to theatre each in their turn and watched them return all drugged up and semi-conscious, after their procedures. I knew it would soon be me, so that Tuesday evening I had a quiet word within my thoughts. The inevitable was going to happen, there is nothing I can do to stop it now, so accept it and get used to it, is what I said to myself. After this self-lecture onwards, I suddenly became quite calm about the whole prospect.

Wednesday morning came and I had to endure the embarrassing experience of an elderly barber shaving my nether regions with a cutthroat razor while joking and laughing with my fellow patients on the other side of the modesty curtains.

"It's OK!" he said. "I'm not nervous!" as he raised the blade while shaking vigorously. Him not being nervous was not the problem, I was shaking with fear as my eyes were fixed on the extremely sharp, glinting silver blade being lowered towards my manhood.

"I've never done it before, but I'm sure you'll be alright, it can't be too difficult," he mused, as the rest of the bay were laughing with great mirth. When an elderly gentleman has hold of your willy, in his thumb and forefinger, held upright at a 90-degree angle and shaving round your testicles with a cutthroat razor in the other hand, it's funny how this sort of thing can focus the mind. Ten o'clock soon arrived and a porter appeared to wheel me down to the operating theatre so Professor Johnson, the surgeon, could carry out the medical procedure. That was that! I can't remember anything about what happened, I just remember waking up back in a bed in ward 27 with tightness across my stomach where the stitches and staples were holding the rather large 12-inch wound together. There was no dressing on the wound, it was left open to the air, with just a covering of iodine. Protruding from the stitched scar was a long tube which led to a concertinaed plastic bottle which I was told was a drain extracting any blood bleeding from the operation site.

I was in hospital for two weeks; in the eighties they kept you in rather than send you home. I was encouraged to walk up and down the ward to help with the recovery process and keep moving rather than lying in bed. One day in the second week a fellow patient said he was going for a walk to see the hospital museum; thinking this was a good idea I agreed to join him. Unbeknown to me, the museum was situated at the opposite end of the hospital, as far away as you could get from ward 27. Off we went, down three floors in the lift, through A&E to a very long main corridor with wards off either side. The corridor must have been at least five hundred metres long. At this point the other guy decided he'd had enough so he informed me he was heading back to the ward. Still not knowing exactly where the museum was, I decided to soldier on, I'd started so I would finish. I continued down the endless corridor, dressed in pyjamas and slippers with a plastic drain emerging from behind my top, swinging by my knee. Eventually after a long slow shuffle which seemed to take an age I arrived at the museum. I was knackered! So much so I didn't have the enthusiasm or stamina to look around the exhibits. I just turned around and set off back to the ward. The return journey was like an expedition; I'm sure Scott must have felt like me as he trudged to the South Pole. How I got back to the ward I don't honestly know, I was on my knees. I was told I should have asked one of the many nurses I passed on my journey if they could get a porter with a wheelchair to help me return, but they all seemed busy, and I didn't want to be a nuisance. On arriving at my bed, I just collapsed into it and slept undisturbed until the following morning. Talk about doing too much too soon, not fully understanding what your body goes through during major abdominal surgery.

The hardest part of the whole process was when I'd been discharged and sent home. I felt like I had been institutionalised, after two weeks on a busy surgical ward to being at home on your own, with every family member at work, isolation, loneliness and the silence while convalescing, was a bitter pill to take. I found myself sniffing handkerchiefs which held the smell of the hospital just wishing I could be back there. I was told I was the youngest person in the country ever, up to that point, to have a cholecystectomy other than car crash victims, so apparently, I was the subject of medical conferences and lectures. Consequently, the medical experts, Prof Johnson and his team treated me with kid gloves, they didn't remove my appendix which they could quite easily have done, as they didn't want to complicate matters with me being a unique case; however, because of this decision my appendix was removed in May 1984, another operation ordeal. They did try a new painkiller on me which made me high as a kite and was fantastic!! Around twenty years later, I bumped into the retired doctors James and Ian. James said to Ian:

"You know who this is, don't you? It's Nathleen's grandson," to which Ian answered,

"Yes, I know, the only patient I diagnosed correctly in 40 years of my medical career." Now there's a thought!!

LONG STAND

I worked at Leeds University in The Department of Textile Industries as a Junior Technician for eight years. It was a job I'd got purely by chance; I started there as a naive and immature 17-year-old on the 16th of July 1979. It was not by a long way the best paid job in the world, but I did enjoy my time there. I worked with the textile designers which was a course of predominately female students all my age. I describe my time there as being a student but getting paid for it. I made some great friends and was invited to many parties and functions with the students. My workplace was located on the ground floor of the Man-Made Fibres Building, which was across the road from the Students Union Building that contained bars, function rooms, shops, a mini supermarket, and the refectory. During the day the refectory was an eating hall which was transformed on many evenings into a concert venue which is where big named bands of the time would perform. Most famously The Who's Live at Leeds album was recorded there. This occurred nine years before I arrived at the university; however, I attended performances by several other bands during my time there, including Judi Tzuke, whom I had the opportunity to meet backstage, The Cure, Snowy White, Lindisfarne, among others.

In the Textile Department I was employed as a Junior Technician to assist my immediate boss Jack Jones during practical lectures in dyeing, finishing and printing of textiles. By far my favourite part was helping the designers screen print their designs onto a ten-metre piece of cloth stuck with gum onto a neoprene print table. My duties included making the screens, ensuring stocks of print binder were plentiful, keeping the colour shop tidy, laying and sticking down the cloth onto the print tables and putting the finished prints into an industrial sized oven to cure the designs onto the fabric so it was permanent. I enjoyed it all.

All these duties were carried out during term time when the students were in attendance, but when the students were away in vacation time there was not a great deal to do. Our responsibilities included cleaning and maintaining the machinery, keeping the area tidy, and performing specific tasks for postgraduate and research students. The summer months could be particularly long and tedious. Occasionally there would be some large project to be carried out in other departments within the Textile Department including Knitting, Weaving, Spinning, Carding, Outdoor Pursuit Research, Library and Research Labs. These large projects might involve rearranging large machines, installing new machines, scrapping old machines, moving academics' offices and other large tasks. When these jobs were in the offing, the technicians from each of the internal departments would be rounded up by the chief technician. His main role was the same as my immediate gaffer, an Academic Related Lecturer in the short staple spinning sheds, but he also had responsibilities over all the technical staff and would gather us together to assist with any of these large projects.

THE WORLD ACCORDING TO ANDY CARTER

Of all the technicians I was the junior, I was the tea boy and of course I was the gofer, Andy gofer this, gofer that, go make some tea and other remedial tasks. As an 18, 19, 20-year-old I thought I knew it all and I thought I'd heard all the jokes played on young junior staff. I was aware of people being sent for glass hammers, buckets of steam and bubbles for the spirit level, I'd heard about being sent to the sandwich shop for buttered ovaries or the sweet shop for a quarter pound of clitoris mints, but on the day in question I was caught well and truly short.

The Textile Department had its own library, a large room full of shelves holding textile-related books, some old even antiquarian, some new and all the theses written by former research students of previous years. At the far end of the library was a partition wall with a door in the middle, it had a frosted window with a name written on it. The door led into an office which was occupied by a specific lecturer who was a strange, aloof character who I never had much to do with; I don't even know what subject he lectured in. This was the summer, of 1981, it was the week Botham's Ashes was taking place at Headingley. The academic was vacating his office, and the technicians were tasked with dismantling the partition wall so the library could be expanded. All the technicians were gathered and led to the library by the chief technician to explain, discuss and plan the job in hand. It was anticipated it would be an easy task; the partition had an aluminium strip framework which supported painted panels bolted to it. The plan was to unbolt each of the panels, remove them from the framework and then dismantle the frame itself. This plan was being carried out with relative success until we reached the panel above the door. The three senior technicians realised this could be the trickiest part of the operation and decided it would be a good time to break for dinner with instruction to meet back in the library at 1400hrs when we would resume the task.

After dinner the technicians reconvened ready to continue with the tricky part of the project. Two technicians were up on step ladders trying to undo and dislodge the panel with another two stood underneath waiting to take the weight once it had been released. As they were struggling up on the ladders, one looked over his shoulder at me and said,

"Andy, go downstairs and see Barry, ask him for a long stand."

Now in my mind's eye this is just what was needed. Remember when you did chemistry at school, and you would set up a stand with a clamp and boss for your experiments. Well, that's what I went to see Barry for, a long pole attached to a stand which would help with the weight of the partition above the door. So off I went leaving the others struggling.

I found Barry in his small office situated at the top of some wooden stairs in the carding shed roof. From the window he had a bird's eye panoramic view of all the carding machines, mule spinners and ring spinners in the shed. I walked up the stairs, knocked on the door and as Barry looked up, I said:

"Hi Barry, they've sent me to see you for a long stand."

"Oh, OK, just go down there by the ring spinner and look around and you'll see it," he said

So, I did, I walked back down the wooden stairs over to the area by the ring spinner where Barry had pointed to. I stood there looking for what was in my mind a larger version of what we used in chemistry lessons at school. Unnoticed by me Barry was watching from the vantage point of his office creased with laughter. I looked and looked, nothing, I couldn't see it by the carding machine, it wasn't by the spinning mule and there was nothing obvious from my position next to the ring spinner. Then Barry came out of his office and stood at the top of the stairs.

"Have you seen it yet?" he shouted across the shed.

"No! Give me a clue, which area is it in?" I answered.

"Oh, just look around a few more minutes and you'll see it," came his reply.

So, I did, stood there like a spare part, scanning the spinning shed for a long pole on a stand. After two or three minutes which felt like half an hour, just as it was becoming ridiculous, and I was getting frustrated and bored, Barry appeared again, descended the wooden stairs, walked over to where I was standing and asked, "Have you seen it yet?"

"No! Come on, show me where it is so I can go back upstairs to help the others."

"Well, have you stood here long enough?" he enquired with a smile in his voice.

BANG!! It hit me like a train, the realisation I'd been had! They had got me hook, line and sinker. I hadn't been sent to fetch a long stand; I'd been sent for a long stand. The Bastards! Apparently the two senior technicians had met Barry over dinner, and this is where the plot was hatched. I trudged back to the library with an embarrassed red face and a bowed head, but by the time I got there I'd recovered and having had a word with myself I also appreciated the funny side. I entered the room with a large grin on my face having accepted I'd been caught out. My colleagues were all laughing when they saw me as I joined in.

I unknowingly had the last laugh in this whole incident, though, because I was the gofer and because I was always sent for the tools, I made it my job to carry most of them with me in my lab coat. So, as they sent me for a long stand, I had disappeared with all the spanners, the adjustable spanners, screwdrivers, pliers and even an electric drill in the large pocket. As I stood by the ring spinner in the carding shed one floor down with all the tools, the other technicians were upstairs, stood under the partition unable to do anything as the tools had disappeared with the Junior as he stood in a different shed for a while doing nothing. Doesn't Karma feel good? These were happy days!

ALL GIRLS TO ALL BOYS

I started work at Leeds University on Monday 16th July 1979 at 0900hrs. I arrived there early and was met by a white lab coated technician who escorted me to the cloth store which would double as an office I would share with my new boss Jack Jones. As I was waiting Jack appeared at the door and greeted me as he took off his jacket, hung it in his locker and donned his own white lab coat, speckled in a multitude of colour. Then he turned round and said,

"Andrew, today you are starting your work adventure whereas I have eight years to do then I'm off!"

I gave a smile and a small chuckle, not really appreciating what he meant. I enjoyed working in the Textile Department from the age of 17 to 26. It was not by a long way the best paid job in the world, but it did have its perks. I was responsible for up to 94 textile designers each year, the vast majority of which were female and all a similar age to me. I was invited to many students' parties, it was like being a student, experiencing the university life and receiving a salary for it. I had access to the student's union, attended concerts in the refectory, in fact as a single man of that age I don't think there were many better jobs. The staff in the department were fantastic, I made some lifelong friends there and we participated in a lot of extracurricular activities.

Another piece of advice Jack gave me early in my career was when he said,

"What you must understand is you now work for an education establishment and all they recognise is certificates. You could have all the experience and knowledge in the world but here in a university it means nothing unless it's written down on a certificate. You may have a degree from a less recognised educational establishment but because the qualification is on a certificate it will take you far." These pieces of information didn't mean a lot to me until one day in 1986.

The university sent me on day release once a week to Bradford College to study for a BTec qualification in Textile Colouration; the department never showed an interest in my progress and gave the impression they were indifferent about my studies, which I did struggle with. I often joke it took me eight years to complete a four-year course, never failing the same year twice, a bit silly and immature really! Consequently, I didn't attain any meaningful certificates. But by 1986 I'd gained seven years' experience in dyeing, finishing and printing of textiles, I knew our department like the back of my hand, I could carry out all the demonstrations, give practical lectures, carry out all the tasks required of me, and was competent in the working of every one of the many machines. Everybody knew Jack was retiring in the September and all including myself assumed I would take over, or so we thought.

It was just another ordinary day in early December 1986 when Jack and I were summoned to see the head of department, in his office. Without knowing the reason, we knocked on his door and entered to find the Professor and

Asad seated at the meeting table. Asad was in my experience a quiet and polite gentleman, he was a slight fellow who hailed from India, my knowledge of his role within the department was very limited as he had a very small office as far away from dyeing, finishing and printing as you could possibly get. This meant our paths seldom crossed, he was just known as the guy who ordered laboratory glass wear, laboratory protective clothing, dry ice and other laboratory equipment. He didn't appear to contribute a lot to the department, as he seemed to be preoccupied in helping his wife run her Indian catering business.

We were beckoned over to join them and as we sat down the Professor explained why we had been summoned to his office. He pointed out that Jack was retiring in September and the department needed somebody to take on the role of carrying out Jack's academic duties, which included the practical lectures we both carried out. As the head of the department, he had decided that between now and September, Jack and I would instruct and demonstrate our duties and skills to Asad so that when Jack leaves, he could take over Jack's responsibilities. Wow, wow, wow, I didn't see that coming, you could have knocked me down with a feather. To describe this as a bombshell does not go anywhere near portraying how I felt. I was devastated and it must have shown because the professor concluded the meeting, told Jack and Asad they could go, but asked me to stay behind.

"You don't seem too happy, Andy?" was his next question.

Pulling myself together with tears falling down my cheeks, I asked, "Am I right in thinking you have just asked me to teach Asad to be my boss?"

"Yes, that's basically it, in a nutshell."

Quickly recovering my composure I managed to ask, "Will I get any more money for doing this?"

"No! You haven't got your college qualifications yet."

I couldn't believe it, Jack was right, experience and knowhow is irrelevant. No certificate, no extra money and a guy who will rely on me to part with my knowledge. After all, Asad did have a degree, but it was nothing to do with textile colouration. That was that, the Professor had made his decision and there was nothing more to say, so I made my exit in a daze. Jack had a lot of sympathy for my situation but admitted there was nothing we could do and after all he was leaving in September.

I left work that evening feeling lower than a snake's belly, the day's events swirling in my mind, shattered that my happy, uncomplicated world had crashed to the floor within a one-hour meeting. I got home, still bewildered, ate my tea, picked up the local newspaper, the Telegraph and Argus, and noted a job advert for West Yorkshire Fire Service. I had applied for a job with the fire service in 1979 when they had informed me, they were not recruiting at that time. In April 1980 the fire service then wrote to notify me they had started recruiting, asking if I was still interested, but of course I was really enjoying my new employment, Jack and I had a fantastic working relationship and what could be better than the student environment I was working within. Although becoming a firefighter was my dream, this was not the right time to be considering a job change – but now, in 1986, after being perplexed and stabbed in the heart by the job I loved, this was the time for a change, so I decided to apply to become a firefighter there and then.

I was sent an application form with instruction for it to be returned by the 12th of December. A couple of firefighter friends helped me with this process, suggesting I wrote out the application form several times in rough so when I did it for real there wouldn't be any mistakes on it. I completed the application and returned it, requesting they inform me it had been delivered. I received confirmation and the information explaining if I hadn't heard from them by 28th February 1987, I should assume my application was unsuccessful. So, think about it, I didn't believe it would take so long before I heard anything, my thought process being, let them get Christmas and New Year out of the way, give them two or three weeks to sift through all the applications I should hear something by the fourth week of January perhaps into the first week in February at the latest. Every morning, I would rush downstairs with eager anticipation to see if the postman had delivered a response, only to trudge back upstairs with head bowed in disappointment. Second week of February, nothing, third week, nothing, by now my rushing downstairs had slowed to a resigned stroll, still nothing. I was starting to convince myself my application was unsuccessful but still hanging on to the fact it was not yet 28th February.

Would you believe it, on the 27th of February I received a letter from West Yorkshire Fire Service inviting me to attend Leeds Fire Station to partake in a series of tests in early May; it also made it clear this was not a job offer and if I was in employment I should not relinquish my current position. This was suddenly very exciting times. The prospect of becoming a firefighter, a job I'd desired since being that ten-year-old cub scout on a visit to Pudsey Fire Station suddenly seemed to be a step nearer. Now the wait was on for May, I knew I had to be at least five foot six inches tall, and I knew I had to expand my chest by two inches. This was accomplished by having an individual hold a tailor's tape measure around the chest with a measurement noted while at rest, and then the tape was allowed to expand as you took the deepest breath possible. If the reading increased by two inches or more, you passed the test. This part of the pending tests was the one I was most worried about, I would ask my mother to hold the tape and read the expansion measurement, I'd achieve, one inch, one and a half inch, one inch again and then one-and three-quarter inches all in the weeks before test day. I could never achieve the magical two-inch target. I'm not sure whether it was down to nerves or not but on the day of the tests I managed to expand my chest by two and a half inches, wow! That was my best, exactly on the day which counted most. My height was not a problem as I was five foot six and a half inches tall – just to make sure I stretched my neck and just lifted my heels ever so slightly off the floor which achieved a height of five foot six and three quarter inches. Job done! We took multiple-choice maths and observation tests, a writing test, and a timed dexterity test assembling fire brigade couplings. The tip for this was to match metal types: metal to metal, brass to brass, etc. My two fire fighter friends had been very helpful in the weeks prior giving me advice and suggestions on how to go about these tests. The written test required me to write a paragraph, two hundred words long, about why you wanted to join the fire service. One of my two knowledgeable friends suggested I practise and practise this task so when it was presented in front of me, I knew specifically what to write and how many words would be in my piece, rather than writing a bit, counting the words, writing a bit more until the target was achieved. My friend's advice saved time, helping me complete the task easily. My other friend who served at Pudsey Fire Station invited me down to show me some of the couplings I would possibly be confronted with on the dexterity test, the trickiest of which was the hermaphrodite coupling used on hose reels; after a bit of practice this challenge was overcome. The two multiple-choice tests were also done with a time constraint and the guy who seemed to oversee the testing process stressed quite clearly and more than once, that we wouldn't be able to complete the whole test in the allotted time. It was explained this was not a problem, when time was called just put your pencil down and stop writing. I think I achieved 36 out of 50. When time was called, I just put my pencil down as instructed. Then the candidate next to me whispered,

"How many did you manage to get done?"

"Thirty-six," I whispered back.

"Oh, I did that many but when he called time I panicked and just filled the rest of the paper in at random."

What a daft thing to do, if after 36 questions he had got 100% and then got the next 14 wrong his 100% would plummet down by 28% to 72%. Ridiculous!! I never saw that candidate again, so I presume he was never offered a job. Having completed the tests at the fire station, we were sent for a chest X-ray at the Leeds chest clinic. We were told we would be contacted by post about whether we had passed or failed and would be informed about the next part of the process, if we had passed. It was also made clear that if we were in employment not to do anything still, as we hadn't been offered a job in the service yet. At this point I happened to mention to a close colleague at Leeds University that I was thinking of joining the fire service. Big Mistake! I confided in him and asked for discretion, but he shared it, making my secret common knowledge. A lesson learnt there, if you don't want anyone to know anything, tell no one!

However, I received a letter informing me I had passed the tests and was invited to attend a formal face-to-face interview at the Fire Service headquarters in September. September was the month Jack was due to retire. The letter once again stated this was not a job offer, and I should not terminate any present employment. Also, most of the Textile Department seemed aware of my intentions which I was not best pleased about. I attended the interview which was in front of two senior officers who asked me a variety of questions. One being:

"If you are successful with this interview and we offer you a post, what would your ambition be within the fire service?"

I thought about it and answered, "As I sit here my ambition is to become the Chief Fire Officer, but if I could just clarify this, as a scout my ambition used to be to become the Chief Scout until I realised the higher up the ranks in the organisation you go, the further away from the scouts and actual scouting you become."

The two officers looked at each other with knowing smiles, and one said, "You don't know how right you are."

And the other added, "What a great answer!"

My chest puffed out as I thought I might have done quite well. The final challenge was a strength test: carrying another candidate in a fireman's lift for 50 metres across the training school's drill ground. Then back to see the officers to be told they would like to offer me a job, but I had to wait until it was confirmed by letter so I should not give notice or leave any current employment. Fantastic! My dream of becoming a firefighter had become reality. I felt ecstatic, a complete contrast to my emotions after leaving the Professor's office ten months earlier. I think I walked round on air with a permanent grin on my face for well over a week.

That was that, all I had to do was wait for my confirmation letter. Jack retired that September and was given the usual bun fight in one of the lecture theatres on the top floor of the Man-made Fibres Building. Shortly after Jack's retirement I was preparing some printing screens in the darkroom when I was confronted by four female designers who appeared quite agitated and anxious. They were about to start their final year and had decided to specialise in printing. Their concerns were that Jack had recently retired, and was it true I was leaving to join the Fire Service? I had to confirm their suspicions as I couldn't lie, to which all four said, "Typical! We're all in our final year of our degree, we pick printing to specialise in, and all the department's expertise is leaving or left!"

They were fuming, but they had a point, so how could I help them with their dilemma? After a thought, I suggested we could spend all the autumn term physically printing, we would print and print, we would make it like a sweat shop so they could get all their designs printed onto fabric. Then in the spring term, after I left, they could focus on studio work, creating colourways, expanding their printed designs and develop their portfolios. They seemed to like this plan, and it was carried out, I was printing with them every spare minute and produced reams of printed fabric. When they received their results, two got first class degrees, one who was aiming for a 2:2 received a 2:1, and the fourth girl who was due to fail ended up with a third. I received a letter from the four of them the following summer, thanking me for the hard work I had put in with them and they said it was that Autumn term which had upped their degree grades. One of the girls who achieved a first went as far to say she dedicated her degree to me as she held me responsible for her success. It was very satisfying and indeed humbling to think my final term with the designers made such a big difference.

Eventually the letter came offering me a job in the West Yorkshire Fire Service. I would start at Training School on 29th December 1987, one year and 21 days since the meeting with the Professor; I received my fire service number and I could now terminate any existing employment. I had a leaving party in The Fenton Pub on Woodhouse Lane attended by most students of that year, and several staff. I was presented with an engraved ink pen by the department, and the textile designers had clubbed together and bought me the LP boxset of Bruce Springsteen Live 1975-1985. They all gave me a great send off.

There is some karma to this story which gave me a wry smile and made me feel quite satisfied, because of the Textile Department's short sightedness, and refusal to increase my pay, they lost all the practical expertise and knowledge in dyeing, finishing and printing in the space of three months. There was no one left who had a clue how to operate the machines, set up the print tables or make the screens, which I don't think the department ever recovered from. Asad, who never fulfilled the tasks asked of him, also left shortly after to join and help his wife with her Indian catering business.

When I left the Textile Department at Leeds University, I was responsible for 94 textile designers, all female and one male. Upon joining the 120th recruits' course at West

Yorkshire Fire Service, I was part of a cohort consisting of 40 firefighting recruits. Thirty-nine were male while one was a female firefighter. So, across the two jobs I went from essentially working with all girls to working with all boys.

THREE DAYS OF HELL!

It was a cold grey Tuesday morning; the rain and sleet fell steadily with very little wind. I left home around 0745 hours, my destination, West Yorkshire Service Training School to join the 120th recruits course. This was the first day of my future fire service career. My emotions were mixed, I was excited and eager to start the job I had wanted since visiting Pudsey Fire Station with the cub scouts as a ten-year-old, but there were also nerves, anxiety and trepidation as I knew from being told training school was going to be tough. During 1987 throughout the application process, I visited Pudsey Fire Station white watch on numerous occasions such was my keenness, I was there that many times I was made to feel like an unofficial member of the shift. It was pointed out to me that training school would be nothing like life on a watch. I was lucky, all I had to do was get through the pending difficult 12 weeks as I knew what being on a watch was like and how good station life could be. This fact was far from my mind as I negotiated the wintery weather to reach my destination.

On arrival I parked the car and headed for the canteen in the training centre. This place was going to be my world for the next three months. I took a seat and joined other smartly dressed, apprehensive-looking men all anticipating what was to come. There was a slight hum but no noise as others joined the group with a nod and the odd good morning. The atmosphere is best described as the first day of a new term at a new school, which we have all experienced, so you can imagine what it was like. Then at 0900 hrs exactly an instructor walked in, he wore a light blue shirt with epaulettes showing two solid bars, Sub Officer markings. He had a red lanyard round his left shoulder, a cap with a red cover, black trousers and highly polished shoes which resembled glass. He introduced himself and proceeded with a roll call. This was done quite calmly with a jocular intent, absolutely no indication of the loud shouting, discipline and intensity which was about to bludgeon into us with great force in the forthcoming weeks.

The morning continued with general admin. Fire Service numbers and ID cards were issued, followed by squad, bed and locker allocation. At 1230 hours we were instructed to muster in the canteen for dinner. This would become the daily routine, breakfast, dinner and evening meal every day for the next 12 weeks except weekend when we would be allowed home. After dinner we were marched to the stores where our uniform and fire kit was issued. We were equipped with four types of attire, workwear which consisted of bib and braces overalls, tee-shirts, steel toe capped shoes and over jacket. Gym wear of shorts, trainers, and track suit. Undress (smart) Uniform which was, Cap, cap badge, Double Breasted Jacket, Shirts with epaulettes, Black Trousers, and Shoes for best which over the weeks would be polished to within an inch of their lives into a mirror glass finish. Finally, our fire kit comprising cork yellow fire helmet, fire tunic, plastic yellow wet legs, boots, sea boot socks, neck chief, whistle, hazmat cards and a three-metre-long personal line. All this first issue was to be kept in pristine condition, correctly ironed trousers, shirts, and overalls. Highly polished shoes, with brushed and polished caps, shiny cap badges and clean fire kit. We were on a recruits course of 50 men of ages between 18 and 30, all with different experiences and knowledge, so to help standardise us all that afternoon we were given instruction on ironing shirts, trousers and tee shirts, and shown how to polish shoes, cap peaks and cap badges. This exercise was all designed to create uniformity with the uniform. Over the pending course we would parade twice a week, Mondays in work wear and on a Friday in undress uniform (best bib and tucker). Both these parades included an inspection; even if your kit was in perfect condition there was always some minor fault picked up on.

After the administration duties and ironing lesson had been completed it was like stepping into a whole new world. We were hit with astonishing force by the weapon with which we were to become accustomed to over the next 12 weeks. All the pleasantries, politeness and respect disappeared as fast as a bullet leaving a gun barrel. Instructors screaming and shouting at us, referring to us as 'rubbing rags' as the sedate well-mannered gentlemen known as training school instructors turned into fire breathing, red faced, angry men using other insults including 'wastes of space' and 'bags of shite'. As a group we were taken to the muster bay and allocated a peg. This was the area which would house our new pristine fire kits. We were ordered to get dressed into fire kit and parade in our squads under the wash outside. Helmet, neckerchief, tunic, seaboot socks, wet legs and boots were all donned at pace. Instructors shouting, "Come on!"

and "Get a move on!" or "Come on, there are people trapped in the fire." As they rattled their batons against the metallic cages, pegs and benches where our fire kit was stowed. These pegs and areas were soon ladened with caps, drill tops and shoes as the recruits exchanged workwear clothing for fire kit. When we were all fallen in outside, we were informed in no uncertain terms it was not good enough, it was too slow, people could have died so you will have to do it again, and we did, again and again and again. It soon became apparent no matter how fast this task was carried out it would never be good enough, even perfection would fall short of the mark.

After an hour of dressing into fire kit, parading and returning to undress and do it all over again we had a tea break. The nervous hum and chatter of earlier had switched into cold, startled shock of the recruits wondering what they had let themselves in for. Remember, I knew what station life was like, but I also knew I had 12 weeks of pain and oppressive bullshit to endure before I reached the promised land. We were taken back down to the muster bay and ordered to change into gym attire. Oh no! Another chance for the subhuman instructors to shout, ball and beast us, and they did. Shouting, screaming and throwing insults, rattling of batons this time against gym wall bars and other equipment. It was relentless, one recruit injured himself doing chin ups and others thought they were at the gates of hell.

At 1700hrs we were released and sent home carrying stocks of uniform, all of which had to be ironed and pressed for the following morning. The end of that first day saw two recruits resign, not being able to take the physical, verbal and mental pummelling we had all suffered. So, all but three retuned the next morning, each recruit now smartly dressed in work wear and armed with coat hangers full of smartly ironed undress uniform. That second morning was in the greater scheme of things quite sedate and palatable, we were marched into the Demo room, which was to become the main lecture area for the rest of the course. The officials from the Fire Brigade Union (FBU) welcomed us and informed us of the dealings of the union. It wasn't a closed shop, but it was made quite clear we should join, and we all did. As the union officials disappeared, the next process changed my future career. All the recruits were sat at single desks when a gentleman wearing civvies, who I had seen throughout the application process, approached me from behind and said,

"Fireman Carter?"

"Yes, Sir," I replied, everyone was referred to as sir.

"Did you have a job before joining the Fire Service?"

"Yes, Sir!"

"Where did you work?"

"Leeds University," I answered.

"Did you have a pension?"

"Yes, Sir!"

"Right then!" He proceeded to pull out of his clutch briefcase a pink A4 form, placed it on my desk, turned it over and said, "Sign here and I'll sort out the rest."

I didn't know what I was signing or why, as there was no explanation, I just complied with what I was told. The answer unravelled some ten years later. I was aware the rule was you had to work till you reached 55 years old to claim the full Fire Service Pension, or if you were over 50 years old with 30 years' service under your belt. Now, after quick mental arithmetic, I joined aged 26 so I could, in my eyes, only reach 29 years' service when I got to 55. So, for the first ten years in the job I was of the opinion I would only receive a 29-year pension. Then after ten years we started to receive annual written pension statements; mine stated I would retire on 31st May 2015. That's only 27.5 years' service, how does that work? Well, it turns out the pink paper I signed in 1987 was, I found out, to transfer my university pension of eight years into the Fire Service Pension which bought me two years and 222 days. This enabled me to retire on full pension after 27.5 years' service at the age of 53! Thank you, to the man with the clutch briefcase.

Dinner followed, then it was back to the muster bay to be screamed and shouted at about how slow and pathetic our changing into fire kit was and how people are dying in a fire due to our snail like inefficient pace, or we'd be sniffing engine fumes as the appliance will have gone by the time you're changed. The fact we would get changed on the fire engines seemed to be omitted from their logic. Half an hour of this bullshit then led us all to the Breathing Apparatus (BA) crawl. An area the size of a small gymnasium, four feet high made into a maze with cage walls. This was the BA training area which would be made pitch dark, you couldn't see your hand in front of your face and could be filled with synthetic smoke. For this exercise we were dressed in full fire kit with a heavy cylinder on our back and a mask on our face. The mask and cylinder were not connected as we'd had no BA training. All recruits were sent round the crawl and up a 30-foot-long sewer pipe to see how they would react to the claustrophobia and darkness. Instructors screaming and shouting in the dark as recruits followed each other on hands and knees through the caged maze making the general atmosphere pressured and stressful. Four more recruits resigned during and after the exercise. This was followed by another gym session as the beasting and shouting continued relentlessly until 1700hrs when we were sent home.

I arrived home as my family were entertaining guests as part of the Christmas celebrations. I felt numb, I felt as if I had been hit by a train and as I sat on my bed in isolation the loneliness, solitude and bewilderment of what I had experienced was overwhelming and tears rolled down my cheeks. You see, the first three days were designed to stop recruits resigning halfway through the live in course. The brigade decided to give the new recruits experience of gym, parading, marching at the double everywhere, taking orders without question, BA claustrophobia and darkness as well as heights, so recruits who couldn't hack it would resign during this period rather than after three, six or ten weeks when thousands of pounds had been spent on training and looking after them. The major problem from my point of view was that we were sent home at the end of each of the three days, on our own, isolated with your own thoughts and experiences. None of your family understood the battering verbally and physically you had been through so couldn't really sympathise. Whereas when we lived in together as a course, if you'd had a bad day on the drill ground the chances are the recruit on the bed opposite would have experienced something similar so it could be talked through with understanding. I think that middle night sat on my bed alone with my family celebrating Christmas downstairs unaware of what I'd been through was probably one of the lowest points in my life.

Anyway, back to it, the following morning I got up having had a serious word with myself to return to the hell hole, stating to Mum and Dad:

"If over the next 12 weeks I say I don't want to go, please make sure I do."

Resignation was not an option for me no matter how hard it got as I would be unemployed, and no way was that going to happen. The third day was more of the same, gym, drill marching, dressing and undressing in and out of fire kit. In the afternoon Bradford Fire Station's Turntable Ladder (TL) and Hydraulic Platform (HP) arrived on the drill yard. Two appliances I would end up loving throughout my career. They came to carry out working at height tests for the recruits. Each recruit was instructed to climb the TL to its full elevation and step off onto the roof of the seven-storey drill tower. I loved it, this was my favourite of the three days, but unfortunately three more recruits couldn't handle the height and resigned.

Although I state training school was a traumatic three months of my life, these three days were by far the worst. Looking back, I suppose I do have a slightly sadistic fondness of the whole experience, but I would not want to go through it again. I have said before I never experienced bullying in the fire service (see Bullying... What Bullying) but the system allowed some instructors to pick on individual recruits. Most instructors were good and ready to help and teach human beings, whereas the odd one or two were just BASTARDS!!

The following Monday after the New Year celebrations, the 120th recruits course started for real. Over the three days induction recruit numbers fell from 50 to 40, which meant we ended up with four squads of ten. All the 40 passed the course and were stationed in the April, the vast majority completing a fully pensioned career, be it all thirty years or less depending on previous pensions being transferred. Training school was an unpleasant but a necessary evil to endure and achieve. It led to the best career anyone could possibly experience! So… Thank you, Bullshitters!

SIR, OR ADO?

My time in the Fire Service was generally a great one, for 27 and a half years it was a laugh a minute. I can't remember any disagreeable or unpleasant times other than the odd trivial fall out with colleagues; twice maybe three times I can recall. Obviously unpleasant jobs could be quite unsavoury, but with these incidents your watch mates would always be there for you. The watches could cope with anything thrown at them, changes to procedures, new policies, or new systems, which would be received with a very negative reaction from the crews, but would soon be adapted and interpreted in favour of the firefighters.

Blue watch always had a cup of tea straight after the daily checks had been completed and prior to the day's drill session. A particular Assistant Divisional Officer (ADO), the officer in charge of the station, did not like this practice so he banned the watch from having a pre-drill cuppa. This decision caused outrage and was met with fury and disdain. So, led by the two Sub Officers, after checks it was decided we would set off and drill away from station, a procedure which was not unusual. In appearance the ADO had won and got his way or so he thought. I don't know whether he found out, but the truth was, we left station, two fire engines, turntable ladder and hydraulic platform to complete in the ADO's eyes a drill session somewhere in the Bradford District. In fact, we took the four appliances to the Hammerton Street café for breakfast and of course a cuppa. This tactic was working well until the morning came when we had just ordered 15 or 16 breakfasts, some full English, some variations and some sausage or bacon sandwiches and a vat of tea. All the bacon and sausage were under the grill; all the eggs were in the pan, and the beans and tomatoes were simmering nicely when we got a fire call. Two pumps, Hydraulic Platform and turntable Ladder were mobilised. This involved every firefighter in the café, eagerly waiting on their morning sustenance, pushing back chairs, and leaving at pace, with comments directed towards the chef explaining we would be back as soon as possible, we just didn't know how long it would be. As it happened it was only a fire alarm actuation in a block of flats, so we were able to return to the café within half an hour.

This ADO seemed to have it in for me as the new recruit on the station. When I was informed I was joining blue watch I went down to the station to meet with them and introduce myself, before I started on the shift for real. While I was there, they were mobilised on a fire call and abandoned me in the mess room staring into my cup of coffee. As I was waiting for them to return the ADO came upstairs to the mess and joined me. He asked if I was the new recruit, which I confirmed, he introduced himself and explained he expected me to address him as Sir, or ADO, just like he expected every other firefighter on the station to do. Embarrassingly for him as blue watch returned from the fire call every one of them passed the ADO saying, 'Morning Robert', 'Morning Rob', 'Morning Bob' and even 'how you doing Bobby?'! As the last member walked past us both heading for the kitchen to continue their interrupted tea break, the ADO sheepishly turned to me and said,

"Of course, Blue watch is a good set of lads, so I do allow them to call me by my first name, but you as a recruit must address me as Sir or ADO!"

After I had served three tours on Blue watch at Bradford Fire Station, I appeared in the Bradford newspaper, The Telegraph and Argus under the headline 'Baptism of Fire' because I had attended 64 fire calls in that short period of time. One of these calls was to Dawsons Cashmere, a large textile factory which had a fire involving one of its huge carding machines. This was my first experience of wearing Breathing Apparatus for real and having to crawl round the carding shed floor, flat on my stomach through pitch black smoke in six inches of cold water caused by the factory's sprinkler system. This may sound silly, but this is what I joined the fire service for, it was hard work, but exciting, exhilarating, scary and brilliant, all at the same time. As was said many times in my career, 'if you don't like getting wet you shouldn't have joined'. As we got control of the fire and the smoke was clearing, we were told to service our BA sets back at the fire engine, then return to the scene to help carry out salvage and damping down duties. I was black right from head to foot, caused by the smoke and sooty conditions, soaked to the skin and cold, but the job needed to be concluded so we just got on with it. The ADO who had appeared at the incident seemed eager to get involved and ended up on top of the carding machine assessing where any hotspots were located. I noticed a small reignition underneath where he was lodged. This small fire was rapidly growing and was becoming very close to burning the ADO's backside. I got hold of a nearby hose reel and started to put water on this small but rapidly developing fire. I felt I had to warn the gaffer of the problem and danger developing underneath him, so I said,

"Bob, there is a fire developing underneath you, be aware."

Even though he was not the most agreeable person I couldn't let him burn. After my words of warning, he spun round and with a look of disdain on his face he snapped,

"Fireman Carter! I've told you when addressing me you refer to me as Sir or ADO."

So bashfully and having been put in my place I continued to put water on the new conflagration which by this time was burning the ADO's arse as it had burnt through his flimsy yellow plastic wet legs. He leapt off the machine with a squeal and a yelp and disappeared away from the incident with everyone in attendance laughing and guffawing with bluster. The Sub Officer shouted at him, "Serves you right, you idiot, the young firefighter did warn you, you buffoon." These comment from my immediate boss made me feel better, you cannot beat backing from your superiors. I did for some time address him as Sir, or ADO but it soon fell away as I became established on the shift.

Firefighters do have a wicked habit of being able to subtly settle a score, getting their own back or teaching someone a lesson. One Friday, before the ADO was to go on his annual leave for 18 days, he intended to have his office decorated in his absence. While he was in his office with the door ajar, a fellow firefighter was stood in the station reception area, tidying fire prevention, fire information, smoke alarm and other leaflets and generally minding his own business.

His attention was attracted to a conversation taking place behind the ADO's office door. The ADO was instructing a contracted decorator of his wishes about the new décor in his office and was overheard saying,

"Leave your wallpaper pattern book with me, I'll have a browse and choose a pattern and leave the book open on my desk with my chosen design on view. Then when I get back from my leave it should all be done to my wishes."

The decorator agreed to this plan, and nothing was imagined could go wrong. The big mistake was to allow that conversation to be overheard.

On return after a relaxing 18 days' leave the ADO returned to work with great excitement and expectation of how his newly decorated office would look. He rummaged in his pocket and got his keys, unlocked the door and was aghast as he was confronted with a visual assault on all his senses, which smacked him between the eyes. The contents of the conversation behind the ajar door had been leaked and some unknown character had entered the office, turned the pages of the pattern book to the most garish, old fashioned, hideous and dull coloured looking paper within the book. The decorator arrived to carry out the work, was by all account surprised by the choice, but thought each to their own as he had often hung wallpaper he did not necessarily like, so wallpapered the office with what he presumed was the ADO's wishes.

The ADO was not happy! But what could he do? He couldn't expect the brigade to pay the cost of any redecoration, he couldn't say anything to the decorator because he was only carrying out instructions and he had no idea whatever who, if anyone, had swapped the page.

The décor was that offensive a future ADO of the station, who couldn't work in the environment, changed offices with the two station clerks who had said they could live with it, and it didn't really bother them. When installed they did hang many pictures and posters on the wall to cover most of the wallpaper. Perhaps a gust of wind had turned the pages of the pattern book was one suggestion put forward as the ADO tried to find out who to hold responsible, possibly one page but more than a dozen, I don't think so he said. The ADO had to live with the distasteful surroundings until he left a few months later to join Wakefield Division. I wonder if he told the Wakefield crews, they had to address him as Sir or ADO?

THE STICK AND THE CHALK

Throughout my 27 and a half years in the Fire Service it goes without saying I saw some very unsavoury sights, but I always found my watch mates would help you deal with these bad experiences. Of course, these sorts of incident did not happen every day, 90 percent of the time fire calls and station life was quite routine. The humour on a fire station was in my opinion fantastic, we laughed and laughed almost every day. You could leave work on the last morning of your final nightshift really looking forward to returning to work four days later because some wind up or practical joke was in continuing motion. It was so much fun even in the times the joke was on me. Not only did you work with your watch colleagues because of the shift pattern, you were living with each other too. Everyone knew everything about each other, and nobody could get away with any idiosyncrasies and habits individuals may have.

Every habit would be picked up on in some jocular way, as previously stated this was seldom done with malice. The farter, the nose picker, the work shy, the miser, the untidy, the snorer, the not so good looking and in one case the smelly. All these habits would be noted and picked upon in some way. Obviously with some of these observations the individual could not do anything about it. The ugly, short, tall even snorer are characteristics which no one has any control over, but the others mentioned in the list are habits which could be remedied with effort and discipline. In my case I was teased about my height (short), my looks (ugly) and my weight (fat), hence I was lovingly referred to as the little fat ugly rat which in my mind was a sign of acceptance and a term of endearment.

In 1987 when I joined West Yorkshire Fire Service there was a height restriction. To join an applicant had to be a minimum of five foot six inches tall. I was five foot six and a half inches tall and said on numerous occasions how important that half inch was. My height was never something I was aware of, similar to most people in society. That was, until I joined Blue watch at Bradford Fire Station. I walked onto the station to meet my new work colleagues, and the first two observations I was confronted with was my lack of good looks and my lack of inches. This was the first time in my life I was made aware of these characteristics. Obviously, this was an issue within the brigade as the first time I went out socially with the watch was to a retirement party at the old Ring 'O'Bells pub in Eccleshill. I was stood with a pint in my hand talking to my watch mates when I became aware of a man and his wife stood at the bar looking me up and down, these actions were very apparent, and it unsettled me. I asked one of my watch members if he knew who it was and what were they doing studying me from head to foot. He told me it was the Sub Officer on Red Watch at Idle Fire Station and they were trying to work out if I was tall enough for the job. Wow! Sobering to say the least.

About three or four tours into my career the HR Department descended onto Bradford Fire Station to carry out the testing process for potential new recruits. The tests included measuring height, expanding chest by two inches, a dexterity test involving couplings and a couple of multi-choice English and maths tests. While we were on dinner break, I was summoned via the Tannoy to the top floor of the station where these tests had been carried out that morning. As I walked through the door into the social room, I was confronted by most of the watch.

"Right then!" said one of the crew. "How tall are you?"

"Five foot six and a half," I replied with confidence, unaware of what I was in store for, "and the half makes all the difference," giving a nervous chuckle.

"OK, we are going to find out once and for all, this is the measuring stick they are using to measure the potential new recruits so take your shoes off and get on it, we will see how tall you actually are."

With nothing to fear, as I was quite confident, I removed my shoes and stepped onto the plate, flat feet and neck slightly stretched just to be sure. As I stood there the audience watched with anticipation as the measure was lowered down onto my head.

"Now then, now then!" I heard the exclamation. "We may have a problem here! It says you are only five foot five and a half inches tall, that's half an inch short of being allowed to join the job."

"Don't be daft." I smiled. "What are you doing?" suspecting some skullduggery but not sure what.

"What do you mean? We aren't doing anything."

"Yes, you are, I'm five foot six and a half," I said trying to defend myself.

"Not according to this stick you're not, let's do it again and we'll stand aside." So, they did, the measure was lowered onto my head and when it was in situ, they all took an exaggerated step backwards. I crouched down from under the measure, so I didn't accidently knock it and lo and behold it read five foot five and a half inches. I was baffled and confused. I couldn't understand how I'd lost an inch in height in such a short time.

Then it started, all the verbal stick and abuse thrown my way.

"How come you're in the job when you're not tall enough?"

"You said you are five foot six and a half and you're not tall enough, did you get in fraudulently?"

As I was still trying to work out in my mind what was going on a member of the HR staff who had been carrying out the tests that morning entered the room.

"Excuse me," one of the watch said, signalling for the individual to come over to where we were all standing.

"Is this the stick used to test the height of any potential new recruit?"

"Yes!" he confirmed.

"Is it accurate?"

"Yes!" he said.

"What happens if a new recruit does not meet the five-foot six mark?"

The member of the HR Team went on to explain, "If anyone fails the height test, they are told they have failed and asked to leave the process."

This was all being discussed as I was staring at the stick, baffled and bewildered, not quite believing what it was telling me, willing it to read five foot six and a half inches.

At this point the banter became a bit more raucous, and robust with venom, as the volume was raised.

"How on earth did you get into this job? You're too short, you shouldn't be here, you must have failed the test, yet you are here!" There were several firefighters around me, as I stood next to a measuring stick, telling me I shouldn't be there.

Then one of the older members of the watch with a very loud and aggressive tone shouted, "You! Ya little shit! My lad is six foot five and as strong as an ox, he applied three times and can't get in yet you, ya little twat, are in the job being too short!"

The fact his son was as thick as a plank seemed to be forgotten and overlooked in his rationale. That was it! I was confused, perplexed and embarrassed. I thought, wrongly, they were trying to get me kicked out of the job. The job I'd worked so hard to get, the job I'd wanted to do since I was a cub scout of ten years old and went to visit Pudsey Fire Station, the job I applied for at 17 knowing I wasn't old enough. The job which meant going through training school, the worst three months of my life. It all seemed to be draining away. The measure was wrong, I knew it was wrong, but I couldn't understand why. I couldn't see a way out, so filling up with tears, trying to hold them back I ran out of the room, I had to get away from the aggressive and harsh humour which was about to shatter my dream.

Seeing my reaction the watch realised they had perhaps pushed me to the edge and to be fair in true fire service style they backed off. When I reappeared from my refuge, they all had their laugh and explained the answer. The reason I appeared to be an inch short was quite simple: they showed me they had put a piece of snooker cue chalk in the slot where the measuring stick attached to the stand. They all knew I was tall enough, they all knew it was a wind up and it did, it wound me up to the hilt. Once it had been explained to me, I thought it was genius. Whoever had thought to put a one-inch piece of cue chalk into that slot was in my view a piece of brilliance!

THE NORFOLK BROADS PART 1

My love affair with the Norfolk Broads started in the summer of 1979. Although I had been aware of the Broads since being a youngster listening in wonder to stories told by Mum and Dad of the two holidays they had enjoyed there, with Auntie Audrey and Uncle Derick the first time and two family friends the second in the 1950s. I was fascinated by these tales of cruising up and down rivers at four miles per hour with the sound of the wash as the craft cut through the calm slow running water, watching the wildlife going about its daily business in natural surroundings, the tranquillity due to the sedate pace and mooring for the evening in the many towns and villages en route, all this sounded enchanting and spellbinding to me. Dad's only criticism was spending time off the cruiser, telling of the time on one of the two holidays he had been on, it was decided they should visit Lowestoft by mooring in the marina at Oulton Broad, catching a bus and spending the day on the beach. Dad's view, which concurs with mine, is 'why would you spend all that money hiring a cruiser which is not cheap, and leave it for a day moored up while you sit on a beach doing an activity you could do any other time of the year by driving a car to the destination and enjoying it then? Surly the point of a Norfolk Broads holiday is to enjoy as much time as you can cruising.

So, in 1979 when Elaine and I were informed our annual family holiday would be to the Norfolk Broads I was beyond excited by this prospect and its reputation. We had hired a boat from the Richardsons boat yard in Stalham called Amber Gem. Auntie Pat, one of mum's gymnastic friends, was coming and could I invite my mate Martin to join us too? Pat Hirst was a petite lady who came across as angry and frustrated with everything in life. She was competitive and very impatient. Being of this firebrand character with a Teflon exterior, she was the sort of lady who never seemed far from a quarrel which caused her volumes of grief and upset. It appeared to me she could have an argument and fall out with herself in a phone box. She still holds the record for winning the most British Women's Gymnastics National Championships with eight titles, yet she smoked like a chimney. This fact I found quite bizarre as she must have spent hours as a top-quality gymnast making her body fit and supple, yet she was destroying it from inside with all the smoke and nicotine she inhaled, and indeed, her heavy smoking eventually led to her demise. She was the first adult I ever heard swear, which was quite a constant within her vocabulary. Never having been married or had any children, she adored Elaine and I very much and always looked out for the both of us. Even though she had this troubled and flawed personality, we both loved her very much in return.

Martin was my mate from school, between the age of 15 and 20 we did a lot together including playing golf, attending concerts and developing into drinking partners. Because there was six of us going on the holiday and only one car,

Martin and I had to get there under our own steam. This entailed us catching a train from New Pudsey to Norwich where Dad would come and pick us up and transport us back to the boat yard at Stalham to rendezvous with the others. The train journey had lasted over five hours, changing at Leeds, Peterborough and Ely, heading to Norwich via March; after three hours or so the journey became very monotonous and boring, but eventually, we arrived at Norwich and met Dad waiting for us.

Amber Gem was a bath-shaped vessel which was detrimental to her manoeuvrability and control, although she was well-designed internally with her own individual characteristics. The engine was governed to keep the top speed at a steady four mile an hour – this in general was not a problem until you were trying to sail against the tide. This was most noticeable when leaving Great Yarmouth travelling north up the river Bure which felt as if we were trying to pedal a push bike uphill or even run through treacle. As the saying goes two steps forward, one step backwards, poor Amber Gem did struggle and as passengers we felt her every endeavour. The wheelhouse was situated in the communal area at the very front of the craft which offered the driver fantastic vision, and everyone could converse and enjoy each other's company within the same cabin; this was also the dining area. The galley was long and narrow and ran down the port side of the boat with bathroom and a bedroom on the starboard side. The chemical toilet was raised slightly higher than an average facility which meant when you were sat on it your legs would dangle – this led to the saying 'I'm off to swing my legs' when any one of us was about to use the amenity. All week turns were taken in driving the boat with everyone having a go, which was a great experience for a seventeen-year-old, but because the craft was shaped like a bathtub and didn't have the traditional pointed bow, manoeuvring it could be tricky. As Dad was supervising Auntie Pat steering the boat he noticed she was drifting towards the bank. After rectifying the problem a couple of times he said,

"Pat, try and keep the boat in a straight line."

She answered sharply, "I am!"

"But you keep steering toward the bank!"

"I know," she said, "I don't want to run over the ducks."

With a slight gasp of frustration and eyes raised to the sky, Dad calmly explained we don't want to run aground, and the ducks would look after themselves. We look back on this incident with great fondness and mirth. The holiday was a success full of fun and laughter, and I had been bitten by the bug. No sooner had we got home, Martin and I decided we wanted more so we booked our own holiday the following year on a vessel which looked the part, Miss More was its name from the Moore boat yard at Wroxham. It had the appearance of the type of cruiser spotted in the Monaco marina, it was a magnolia colour with a high cockpit and reclining area at the rear which had a brown canvas cover; when in use this was very pleasing, and colour coordinated to the eye. From the raised steering position two or three steps led down into the dining and galley area, then beyond past the toilet and shower room into a double cabin with two single beds. The dining area was on a night converted into its own double birth. The craft itself had a real touch of class and style about it.

Although the boat in 1980 was all we wanted, the holiday itself was not the best. Not because of The Broads surroundings, or the weather, it was more to do with my fellow crew. Martin and I were drifting apart with our friendship; I hasten to confirm there was no animosity, it was just a simple case of leaving school, going to college and finding new friends and colleagues at work. The holiday was all booked when a few months prior Martin had asked if he could bring his mate from college along for the holiday, a guy I had met on several occasions. Foolishly I agreed, and leading up to the trip there was no suggestion of what I would experience over the forthcoming week. The saying 'two's company, three's a crowd' was quite appropriate for what I endured. The first indication of things to come was when we were handed the boat at the yard, and without any discussion I was told the other two were going to have the front double cabin and I would be in the dining area and galley at night, so separation was instigated from the start. Having said that, a highlight of the holiday was when we sailed into the Norwich Yacht Station passing Carrow Road, Norwich City's football stadium, which was very impressive looking at it from the river. It was Easter Monday, and we realised it was the day of the East Anglian derby between Norwich City and Ipswich Town. This was too good a chance to miss, so we bought tickets and attended the game. Norwich surprisingly won, one nil with Justin Fashanu getting the only goal from right in front of us. It was probably the best day of the whole holiday with all three of us getting on well. For the rest of the remaining holiday, I felt like it was them against me. Martin was influenced by his mate who had not experienced this type of holiday and basically wanted to do nothing, not muck in and naturally seemed to go against everything I suggested with Martin backing him up from behind. At the end of the holiday we had to get up early to return the boat back to the yard – this was agreed the night before – but in reality I was the one who got up, untied the boat, struggled with the portable TV aerial which had fallen overboard while still attached as the other two lay in their beds laughing and giggling like schoolchildren at my difficulties. For three quarters of an hour, I was akin to a single yachtsman navigating down the river until guilt got the better of them both and they raised their heads out of the cabin. Martin's mate was in general an all-right kind of guy, but he was a bit like medicine, acceptable in small doses! I found trying to be a friend of your friend's other friend was quite tiresome, frustrating and somewhat futile. I think the general atmosphere on the boat could best be described as tolerating each other. I don't think I have ever met the bloke since that holiday, which is not something I have missed.

Once again for this holiday, we had travelled to Norfolk by train, the journey seemed easier due to Martin's and my previous experience plus of course there was three of us. The end of the line this time was Wroxham Station from where we could walk across the main road straight into the boat yard. After a week of glorious April sunshine, we made our way home, and as we left the boat behind, I rang Dad from a phone box in Wroxham asking if he would pick us up from Leeds Railway Station, giving him the estimated time of arrival – no mobile phones in the early eighties. His response to my query was quite surprising.

"I will if I can get out," he said.

"Get out?" I queried with bewilderment in my voice. "What do you mean, get out?"

Apparently, he went on to explain, while we were in Norfolk experiencing nice warm spring weather, Pudsey and West Yorkshire had been the victim of a large deposit of snow, meaning Dad was unsure about his ability to get the car up the notoriously difficult hill in icy conditions, and out of Hillfoot Drive. Coincidentally, one of the residents on the estate knew a man with a JCB who came and cleared the problem. If it hadn't have been for this good Samaritan, Dad would not have been able to pick us up. Although the atmosphere and companions on this holiday were not particularly amiable, the experience of the Norfolk Broads shone through, and I had overall a second tremendous holiday.

Then came The Norfolk Broads 1982, I had been waxing lyrical about how good a holiday cruising round the rivers of Norfolk was to anyone who would care to listen. This struck a chord with my cousin Jim, who I played rugby with, and he decided he would like to experience it for himself. Not being one to discard the chance of another of my rapidly emerging favourite holidays, we got our heads together and booked a fine-looking boat named 'Skipper' from the Broom boatyard in Brundell, just outside Norwich. We picked this boat because everything was inside, it had a roomy wheelhouse which contained the dining and relaxing area, the galley and the walkway past the shower and toilet suite into two single berths in the front cabin. Outside at the rear, through a set of patio doors was a sundeck with a fixed table to eat from through the day and on an evening, on top was plenty of space to sunbathe and a great vantage point to observe the river wildlife. Skipper was a well-designed, small but spacious and speedy craft which when we saw it physically, we were thrilled and looked forward to the pending week of relaxation in minor luxury. The excitement and anticipation prior to the pending holiday must have been infectious as it was all we could talk about among our fellow rugby teammates. So much so two of them, Dean and Steve, decided they might like to join us for the same week on their own boat. After discussions they decided to book Miss More due to my recommendation, and from seeing photographs I'd showed them from my previous holiday.

Jim owned a red Mk II Ford Escort, and the plan was to drive down to the boatyard to pick the boat up then we would meet Dean and Steve somewhere on the river the following day. We arrived at the boatyard in good time and was told our boat wasn't quite ready for us so to remove the four-and-a-half-hour journey out of our system we went to the local pub to kill time with a couple of pints and a game of pool. As we were playing, we became aware of an elderly gentleman sat at the bar watching us, and after a while he enquired where we hailed from.

"By the sound of your accents you're not from round these parts, are you, where have you come from?" he enquired.

"Leeds, West Yorkshire," I replied.

"I thought I detected a deep Yorkshire twang within your dulcet tones. Are you here on holiday?"

"Yes, we are just waiting for our boat to be ready at the boatyard across the road."

"Well, I'm from Castleford myself, but I live down here now and have been for the last five years."

Then he proceeded to tell us why he had moved out of West Yorkshire and into Norfolk, and his reasons took our breath away. He proceeded to explain with some misplaced pride and satisfaction. His attitude was to say the least aggressively racist and quite nasty, comments which offended both of us and comments which could lead to one being arrested for today. It turned out he was not a very pleasant chap, so we finished the game of pool, drank up, and went off to pick up the boat.

After being shown round the craft and its workings, we set off down the river in glorious sunshine and eventually moored up and spent our first night at Reedham, a small village just southwest of the large inland estuary called Breydon Water. The following morning, we got up, had some breakfast and cast off, heading south towards Beccles. As we were cruising at a leisurely pace down the River Waveney, I noticed a cruiser behind us which I recognised. Incredibly, it was Dean and Steve aboard Miss More, what a great sight it was to see two of our rugby mates steaming after us and to join us on what at the time seemed to be a holiday of a lifetime. The rest of the week was spent together as a four on two boats, we had water fights, raced across Breydon Water where there was no speed restrictions, at an eye watering seven miles an hour, attended many pubs, stopped overnight at a secluded wood and experienced other water-based activities. The holiday was fantastic, the weather was hot, the food and drink on and off the boats was excellent, and the result of this experience strengthened my resolve and love affair with the concept and area of The Norfolk Broads.

So, you can imagine my delight when, in 1983 I was informed the annual holiday with Uncle Dougie, Auntie Rosalie and cousins Tania and Craig, which had become tradition since the early 1970s, was to be on The Norfolk Broads. In previous years the eight of us had been on holidays to Southport, Bridlington, The Isle of Man, Llandudno and Newquay to name but a few. So, after what I was led to believe took some persuading of Auntie Rosalie, Dad booked us all for a week on the boat Flash of Light, an eight-berth craft from the Herbert Woods boatyard at Potter Higham. This was brilliant for me, a bit of a bonus really, I looked at it as an extra week enjoying my favourite holiday. Flash of Light was a stunning boat, it had six berths plus two to be made up in the wheelhouse, two bathrooms and had some very attractive lines and looks, all in all very impressive. The configuration was Elaine and Tania had the front cabin; Craig and I were in the stern, Mum and Dad had their own central cabin, while Dougie and Rosalie slept in the wheelhouse.

At this period of my life I was a heavy smoker, as were Rosalie and Dougie, and from being legally old enough we would hide from Mum and Dad and share a crafty cigarette out of their sight while on our holidays together. On the Norfolk Broads holiday we would sit at the rear of the boat covertly and smoke. It was on one of these occasions Rosalie eventually persuaded me to come clean and admit my habit to Mum, a vocal anti-smoker, something which I'd successfully hidden from her for a couple of years. This took a lot of courage, and I was full of apprehension and guilt as I approached her cabin door with anxiety and nervousness. I felt like a schoolboy stood outside the headmaster's office about to admit responsibility for some mild juvenile misdemeanour. I hesitated before knocking on the door; 'here goes' I muttered to myself.

"Come in," I heard the response.

As I entered, I was confronted with Mum sat on her bunk dressed in a blue tracksuit, knitting.

"Hello, son, are you ok?" she enquired as she looked up from her clicking, moving needles.

"Yes," I said, "I'm fine, it's just that I have something to tell you!" I had reached the point of no return, admitting there was something on my mind was where I had to follow it through.

"I've come to tell you that I smoke!"

The disappointment on her face was evident; perhaps this was not the time or place to inform the most important person in your life this piece of news which went against all her beliefs and lifestyle. Her reaction was unnervingly quiet and matter of fact. She just seemed to accept the information as if she already knew, there was no bollocking or reprimand, just an overwhelming expression of disappointment with my declaration. Quite calmly and quietly she conveyed her feelings and pointed out the harm I was doing to myself, all of which I was aware of. The fact that I enjoyed smoking was in Mum's eyes no defence. All in all, it was a relatively short encounter which lifted the heavy burden off my shoulders, it all ended with both of us expressing our love for each other as I turned to exit the cabin. That was it, deed done, I went back to see Auntie Rosalie and told her of my confession. She said she was proud of me as she knew it couldn't have been easy, but it would be for the best in the long run. I must admit these words of praise and support did not ease the guilt I was feeling. Nevertheless, we both disappeared to the stern of the boat and enjoyed a cigarette together.

Other than the day of admission, the holiday was fantastic, and the boat Flash of Light was even better. All our plans came to fruition, we visited Coltishall, Stalham, Reedham, Beccles and Norwich to name a few. We were able to moor quite easily at all these places and had some lovely evenings together. All too soon the holiday concluded and on the journey home I had decided it wouldn't be too long before I returned to once again experience this style of holiday in one of the most picturesque and beautiful areas of the British Isles. Not knowing how soon that would be with its own trauma.

To be continued!!

NORFOLK BROADS PART 2

Having experienced four fantastic holidays on the beautiful Norfolk Broads, I felt the time had come to spread the word, so in 1985 I thought it might be a good idea to take my scout troop there on a boating holiday which would double up as their week's summer trip. This annual trip had in the past included attendance at scout jamborees and camping in different locations around the country, but boating for a week would be quite unique and thrilling. I discussed my proposal with the patrol leader's council, the older scouts, and they took it on board (pardon the pun) and seemed quite excited by the prospect. Having received the go ahead from the scouts, I needed to know if there was any policy or rules to follow from the Scout Association's point of view about taking a group of scouts on this type of adventure. I phoned the Assistant District Commissioner for General Duties (ADC GD), who was a very experienced scout leader whose knowledge of this type of event was encyclopaedic. He assured me all was in order, and because I was booking it through a holiday company, they would cover any insurance needs within the cost of the boat hire. I assembled a team of leaders, John, Jonny, Liz and Colin, gathered names of boys who were interested, chose the dates, the last week in August, picked two identical boats, the eight-berth Flash of Light from Herbert Wood's yard, drew up the week's programme, wrote the menu, and enquired about the possible means of transportation. With all these costs calculated, I started to collect the money from everyone to pay for the holiday. The total bill being £2000, equating to £125 for each attendee, which for a seven-day holiday seemed quite reasonable and inexpensive.

With about two months to go before this stimulating prospect, and the boys' anticipation and excitement levels growing with each passing week, I received a phone call from the very bombastic, it's my way or no way, dictatorial District Commissioner, the head of the Pudsey District Scouts. I picked up the ringing phone.

"Hello."

"Is that Andy Carter?" he asked with a monotone, emotionless voice.

"Yes, speaking."

"It's the District Commissioner here."

"Oh yes, how are you?"

"Yes, I'm ok, but I am not ringing to tell you about my health, I understand you are intending to take your troop of scouts on the Norfolk Broads, are you?"

"That's right, the last week in August, 11 scouts and five leaders," I answered with pride, pleased with myself of how I had dealt with this large logistical project.

"I'd heard so, and who holds the charge certificate?"

"Who holds what?" I retorted, not quite understanding the question.

"The charge certificate, it's the formal certificate acknowledging that there is a qualified leader within your group who has proved competence in leading boys doing water activities; it also covers insurance requirements."

Never having heard of a charge certificate, I admitted, "Nobody holds a charge certificate," so he came back quite abruptly with "You're not going then, are you?". I was flummoxed, gobsmacked and dumfounded all at the same time, a shattering shiver went down my spine, I'd two thousand pounds invested on this holiday and here was a man who seemed to be having great delight and satisfaction at informing me we could not go. There was no suggestion of a solution, or advice on how we could achieve one; in fact, there was no help coming from the other end of the phone, other than he wouldn't allow us to go. I tried to defend myself, explaining I had asked the ADC GD who had said the holiday company would cover any insurances. The reply was, "Well, he's wrong!"

That was it, the line went dead, I was sat on the bottom step with receiver in hand and dialling tone buzzing in my ear, shell shocked, stunned and numb.

Immediately I replaced the receiver, then phoned my Group Scout Leader for advice.

"Hi Kev, you'll never guess what that bastard has just told me."

"Which bastard?"

"The DC, he's just informed me I can't take the kids on the Norfolk Broads, there is two grand paid on it and ADC GD said it would be ok because of the holiday company's insurance policies."

"What are you doing now?"

"Nothing!"

"Right, I'm coming round, we'll go see him."

So we did; as we arrived at the DC's house who did we bump into just leaving but the ADC GD. I wound the car window down.

"Hi, mate, you said we didn't need anything from the scout association to enable us to take the kids on the Broads."

"You don't, the holiday company covers everything."

"He says, that's a load of bollocks and we need a charge certificate!" as I gestured to the DC's house.

"Well, he's wrong! You don't need a charge certificate if you are using a commercial holiday company for your trip, I've done it more than once!"

"Can you come and tell him that, now?"

"No, I've got to get off, I'm late as it is!" and off he went.

We entered the DC's house, and it was as if he was expecting us, he had a copy of the POR (Policy, Organisation and Rules), the scout rule book, commonly referred to as press on regardless, open at some random page where the smallest sentence ever conceived referred to the fact that 'charge certificates' are required for water activities. Once again, he informed us it had to be accepted as read because this is the rule. I tried my best to argue my corner and protect the holiday, but he was adamant the rule was the rule, and we wouldn't be going. I left the house in a daze, it looked like the holiday was doomed, his parting comment was he would investigate it, which was at least a thread to hold on to.

Across the following fortnight very little sleep was had as the worry about the pending holiday and with all that money hanging by the balance. The possibility of disappointing the boys, losing most of the money, and having to cancel the holiday significantly affected my well-being, and it didn't seem fair. This situation had arisen due to a decision made by a scouting official, who was adamant we were not authorised to attend. I was so distressed that I seriously considered packing in scouting and having nothing more to do with the organisation, which could allow me to take the group away on the Norfolk Broads privately and without the DC's pathetic permission and reasoning. Eventually I received a phone call from the elated DC, concluding that he had solved my problem, yes, I thought, the one you'd created. We could go on the holiday but while there we would have to meet up with a member of the Broadland Scout District, who held a charge certificate, to confirm our procedures and rules on board were safe and to a high standard. I asked John, if he would carry out this responsibility which he willingly agreed to. He arranged three different meetings during the week's holiday, with this representative, who never showed up to any, meaning all this strife and worry caused by the dictator of a DC was pointless. The DC seemed to get great joy and satisfaction out of creating a problem, then solving it and receiving all the accolade and praise, total bollocks!

The day arrived full of excitement and anticipation, scouts being dropped off by parents and leaders buzzing around loading rucksacks, food and minimal equipment into the transport. We had hired an old bread van from a scout group in the neighbouring district, who had a marching band and used two buses and the van to transport their members and instruments to competitions and displays around the country. Admittedly the van had seen better days, but we were assured the trip to Norfolk would be well within its capabilities. With scouts sat on benches down each side and rucksacks stored down the middle, we set off Norfolk-bound. Scouts, John,

Colin and Liz in the van, and me and Jonny in his small work's Mini Metro van, stacked with bags and coolboxes of food and luggage to help vacate more room for the scouts. The plan being the car would follow the van all the way down to Potter Heigham. We had got as far as junction 39 on the M1, two miles short of Woolley Edge Service station and 32 miles into the 186-mile journey. The van entered the shaded area, a neutral zone where the junction merged with the southbound carriageway. Theoretically it was stranded in the middle of the motorway with the junction coming up over our left shoulder and the motorway, with cars traveling at 70mph on our right, scary. Jonny positioned us behind the van as thick black smoke billowed from the engine compartment. It was obvious this knackered old van wasn't going any further that day. Jonny and I headed to the service station to phone the representative of the neighbouring scout group who instructed us to ring the RAC, no mobile phones in 1985. We did this and returned to the stricken vehicle. My main concern was the safety of the boys, even though they were well shielded and protected in the van within the chevroned area. A police traffic vehicle stopped and asked us what the problem was, they were concerned but happy the RAC were on the way and instructed us to get the van moved off the motorway as soon as possible. The RAC arrived relatively quickly only to inform us the van was caput and it was too heavy for his transit van to tow us the two miles to the service station. Wow, what do we do now? We seemed to be stuck, and the whole holiday was in jeopardy. Eventually, being sympathetic to our plight, the RAC man agreed to tow us very slowly off the motorway to the relative haven of the services.

The stay on the service station lasted a hell of a lot longer than anticipated – five hours to be exact. It was obvious the van could not be fixed so we needed a contingency plan. At least we had public payphones available, toilets and plenty of expensive food and drink to refresh and sustain the boys. Colin phoned his father, asking if he could go to a local Leeds van hire firm, book a minibus and rendezvous with us on the service station to enable the journey to continue. His father did this willingly, but it all took time. As he left his house with the acquired van, he spoke to his neighbour saying, "I've got to go sort my lad out, he's stuck on Woolley Edge service station with a load of scouts on their way to the Norfolk Broads; Woolley Edge, that's Sheffield, isn't it?"

"Yes," replied his neighbour, which resulted in him driving straight past Woolley Edge at Wakefield to Woodhall Services at Sheffield a good 30 miles further south. He discovered his mistake on arrival at Woodhall, so he had to travel further south to get onto the northbound side and drive past Woolley Edge to junction 39, go round the roundabout and return to us on the southbound side of the services. To address the scouts' boredom, we engaged them with board games, card games and reading. Additionally, Dire Straits had recently released their Brothers in Arms album which was constantly played on the Mini Metro's CD player at a volume we could all hear. Every time I hear a track off that album it takes me back to the nightmare of Woolley Edge. Eventually Colin's father arrived, and we went through the process of transferring kit and equipment into the smaller Transit minibus, we had to sit the scouts in the minibus and stack the rucksacks and bags around them, I felt sorry for the boys because the long journey must have been purgatory, being tightly packed in with very little wiggle room. From the rear, the minibus appeared to be near overloaded as we noticed it was very close to the ground, but needs must. The new plan was Jonny and I would set off to the boatyard and get there as quickly, and legally, as possible, board the boats and wait for the rest of the group to arrive. We had informed the yard of our unfortunate delay, to which they confirmed this was not a problem, the boats were ready and waiting for us in the marina so we could board them, spend the night on board and then set off on our cruising the following morning.

The following morning, we woke up, fresh and excited after the previous day's shenanigans, and Colin's father returned to Leeds with the minibus, as we commenced the holiday, with the concerns of the previous day turning into casual reminiscing. We had decided after discussions and checking of the tide times at Great Yarmouth, our best plan was to head to Beccles, the most southern point of the Broads, and spend the rest of the week working our way back up north. I would be skippering boat one and John would skipper boat two, so as breakfast was being served the voyage began. The weather was fantastic, wall to wall blue sky and very warm temperatures. We navigated Great Yarmouth and Breydon Water with ease and no incident. The rule was that all personnel wore a life-jacket when moving around the outside of the boat, but if they were sunbathing or inside this rule could be relaxed. As we left Breydon Water, a life jacket from boat number two blew into the river. The boat had to turn around to retrieve it with a boat hook, causing much laughter. Then because we were determined to get to Beccles in quick time, boat two was stopped by the river police and warned about speeding; once again this induced great mirth amongst the boys as they witnessed one of their leaders, John, receiving a ticking off by the authorities – they never had a word with me piloting boat number one. We cruised under St Olaves road bridge and Somerleyton rail bridge, making great time to arrive in Beccles for tea.

Just as we were passing the Waveney River Centre my attention was drawn to John who was piloting boat two, I slowed so he could come alongside where he informed me his throttle cable had snapped, and he couldn't put the boat into reverse. Oh no! Now what? While floating down the river we had a quick cross boat conflab and decided to moor at the centre for the night and phone the on-call mechanic back at the boatyard to come and mend the cable. At the Waveney River Centre boats are required to moor stern on, so watching John trying to carry out this manoeuvre with no reverse gear was one of the funniest things I have witnessed. The plan was for me to moor my vessel then catch ropes thrown from the stern of John's vessel and manhandle it into the moored position. This proved to be more difficult than what it sounds. We attempted this several times and eventually gave it up as a bad job, so it was decided to drive it in bow first and secure it to my boat and another already moored up on the other side. We did laugh and felt slightly embarrassed as fellow holidaymakers would look and comment on the fact the boat was moored the wrong way round. The mechanic arrived first thing the following morning to mend the cable, sarcastically commenting

"You should moor boats stern on, not bow forward!"

To which I answered with equal sarcasm, "You try doing it with no reverse cable!"

He realised his foolish comment and we ended up warming to each other. The repair job didn't take long, and both boats were soon on our way heading to Reedham; we never did get to Beccles.

Reedham is a charming Norfolk village and was the first location John had arranged to meet with the man holding the charge certificate, but he never showed up. There is a long waterfront setting where we moored the boats and for the late afternoon activity we took the scouts on a small hike round the surrounding countryside, which built a great appetite for tea. The boys had been told to bring the odd board game for the evenings to keep us entertained. One scout brought a game called Poleconomy, a high business game involving mergers, acquisitions, takeovers and bankruptcy of massive fictional businesses; this became a firm favourite with us all. Most evenings, all 16 of us would gather in the boat's wheelhouse and play this game late into the night, enjoying plenty of laughter and fun, while consuming snacks and drinks.

The next morning, we headed up the River Yare to Norwich where a second meeting with the man holding the charge certificate was arranged; again he never showed up, patience was wearing thin. Without a set plan, the leaders met to discuss potential activities. Liz who was the holiday treasurer and first aider pointed out we had saved money due to the old bread van breaking down and the hiring of two minibuses to get us to Wroxham and back, so suggested we might take the boys to the pictures to see the newly released Teen Wolf movie. The weather had turned, and this would be an activity we could afford to do and would keep everyone out of the rain. Upon our arrival in Norwich, we located a cinema near the yacht station, reviewed the relevant showtimes, and took the scouts to see the film which was targeted at younger audiences. The boys enjoyed the movie; the adults endured it. All the scouts throughout the holiday took turns driving the boats while being supervised by a leader, they really enjoyed this part of the experience. On the journey up the Yare one scout got his bearings completely wrong and collided with a manmade landing with quite some force. On impact there was a loud shrill scream echoing from deep in the cabin area toward the bow of the boat. On investigation the squealing noise came from Liz who was using the chemical toilet and as the boat impacted the landing stage with a bump, the blue chemical within the toilet had splashed back, covering Liz's backside – she wasn't too pleased as she ended up with a blue stained arse for the next couple of days. Yet another incident which caused great laughter, even Liz eventually saw the funny side. At least there was no damage to the boat after the collision.

The following day entailed a lengthy cruise, as we made our way northward to Stalham. This journey included returning across Breydon Water, passing through Great Yarmouth, and navigating up the River Ant, a voyage expecting to take approximately ten hours. We set off from Norwich before 0700hrs which coincided with low tide at Breydon Water and Yarmouth, and ensuring we had time to reach our destination. During the leisurely cruise, we enjoyed sunbathing, water fights, and occasional races along the quieter waterways, the scouts loved it and had a great day. We arrived in Stalham and moored the boats, anticipating a good tea and another game of Poleconomy. As we were playing the game with loud excited voices fully focused on the strategies, we heard someone shouting from outside. It was the Broadlands District Commissioner coming to inspect what on land would be referred to as a campsite. I'm not too sure what it is referred to involving two hire craft, but that is the gist. When you take a group of scouts camping outside your district, you must complete a PC (Permission to Camp) form to inform the hosting district of your stay. The host DC will then give you a surprise visit to inspect the conditions, and procedures, fill in a report and send it back to your home district. He indicated his approval in his report on our return, stating how he was extremely impressed with the cleanliness, leader responsibility, the programme planning, the menu, chore rota, and the manners, morale and general good humour of the scouts. It was the most favourable camp assessment form I had received during my 20 years as a leader. I made sure our pompous, self-centred and pretentious DC knew what the Broadlands DC had to say about the holiday he had tried to cancel.

Due to our delay at the start of the holiday, we felt we had lost a night, so to compensate for this we decided on our final night instead of spending it back in the boatyard we would go to Wroxham. This meant we would have to be up early the following morning to enable us to return the boats to Potter Higham before 0900hrs on the morning of the last day. The scouts agreed with this plan, especially when we informed them John and I would get up, set off on the journey while they were all still in bed, an experience attractive to any teenager. Wroxham was the third attempt to meet the guy with the charge certificate which now seemed to be rapidly becoming a total waste of time, especially as the DC had inspected us the previous evening so when he didn't appear we gave it up as a bad job, realising the trauma and worry caused by our DC was regrettable, futile and pointless… Pillock! The evening in Wroxham was eventful – we decided to give the scouts a free run so they could let off a bit of steam before the pending long journey home the following day. Before they were released that evening into the unsuspecting town, the message was instilled into them to remember who they represent, be on their best behaviour, stay in numbers above two and not create any disturbance. I was very confident that they would comply to these rules as in past experiences the scouts had never let me down. As the leaders wandered, we found our boys playing football, using the adventure playground, exploring the town and buying gifts for their families back home. Regrettably, a couple of the senior members of the group discovered a licensed disco and spent most of the evening there. Although they returned to the boats before curfew, their noticeable intoxication was evident and observing them manage their hangovers the following morning was another source of amusement.

We faced a dilemma the next morning about when to start our return journey to the boatyard. With an estimated travel time of four hours, we needed to leave before 5:00 am. John and I would get up, leaving the boys in bed, but because of the early hour we would have to be extremely quiet, so we didn't disturb other boating holidaymakers with noise and wake vigorously rocking their boats. Our first challenge was to get through Wroxham Bridge which was very tight. You can't go through these days without a pilot, but in 1985 you could do it yourself. I went first and was quite proud of my attempt as the boat never touched the sides. John wasn't so lucky and noisily scraped the boat down one side followed by a scream of elation as he had managed to get through. I turned round and shushed him because we were trying to be silent. The rule was, when we were passing boats and villages, we would keep to the speed limit but in open river we could put the throttle down and speed up.

We left it close as we arrived at the boatyard at 08:50, marking the conclusion of a wonderful holiday filled with remarkable experiences. Despite the problems and setbacks thrown at us, I felt a great sense of accomplishment and pride in my ability to successfully manage and overcome the challenges that arose, along with a great team of fellow leaders, so thank you, John, Jonny, Liz and Colin. The last task was to transfer the gear and equipment from the boat and into the hire minibus which had been driven down by one of the parents. The boys were instructed to board the bus once more, and subsequently, all items were carefully loaded around them, and with Jonny's Mini Metro van filled to the brim. The journey home was full of joy as everyone recalled incidents on the holiday and the exciting prospect of meeting up with parents and loved ones. This expectation seemed to make the four-hour journey feel quicker than it should have done, and our homebound destination was achieved when we saw the group of friends and relatives waiting for us outside the scout hut. This was not the conclusion though, as all the gear and equipment needed to be unloaded, the minibus returned, and thanks from parents received. Eventually all the leaders ended up in the pub to relax with a pint and reminisce with missed partners, telling tales of laughter and incidents aboard the two Flash of Lights. This was also the night I had told all my peers I would be packing in smoking, and I made up for this fact as I lay back, mentally assessing my achievement and inhaled on my last ever cigarette. Andy, I thought, you have given those teenage boys fantastic and unforgettable experiences, as I looked up to the ceiling while exhaling smoke with a great sense of self-satisfaction. Still to this day I get stopped by boys from that holiday, who will all be now over 50 years old, telling me how great that holiday on the Norfolk Broads was. Some admit to taking their own families because of that introduction. Little do they realise how close it came to not happening at all!

BULLYING!
WHAT BULLYING?

I left West Yorkshire Fire Service Training School in March 1988 to join Blue Watch at Bradford Fire Station on Nelson Street. The Brigade made a last-minute change, and I was moved from Green Watch at Bingley Fire Station where I'd been assigned the previous Wednesday. One hour before I was scheduled to leave for the fire station to report for duty, I was instructed to report to the station officer's office, where I was informed that I would now be going to Bradford. After telling me this news, the station officer concluded,

"You'll be very pleased with that then?" to which I replied,

"Actually no!"

His reaction was one of surprise, disbelief and anger. Why would a recruit not want to go to Braford Fire Station? The jewel in the crown of West Yorkshire Fire Service.

My reaction stemmed from when I had applied for the job 15 months earlier. As part of the application process, I asked my best friend's father, who had known me for many years, if I could put his name down as a character reference referee, he said he would willingly oblige. He and his wife owned two burling and mending businesses in Bradford, employing firefighters part-time. They regularly attended social events at the fire station, becoming well-acquainted with the firefighter's role. This made him seem ideal for the job. Although he was willing to do the reference, his wife said,

"I don't think the fire service is for you, I know of the bullying that takes place at Bradford Fire Station, and I don't think you'll be able to cope with it."

This comment did concern me, so much so that as I started my career I would say 'I'll serve anywhere in West Yorkshire apart from Bradford'. She had inadvertently painted a dark picture of the place and personnel. So, when I was informed I was going to Bradford rather than Bingley, I went cold and was filled with trepidation, I really didn't want to go to Bradford. I was told by all the training school Sub Officers it was the place to be as I would have the pick of any fire station in the Bradford Division because every firefighter wished to get transferred into Bradford, so I would be able to transfer out with great ease. As I left Training School heading down Wakefield Road to report for duty at Bradford Fire Station, I had a serious word with myself. Why was I taking notice of the words of an elderly lady when everyone in the know was telling me it was the best posting I could possibly wish for. I later described the transition from Bingley to Bradford as akin to winning the lottery, so much so that I spent my entire 27-and-a-half-year career at the prestigious Bradford Central Fire Station.

I can honestly say with hand on heart I never experienced being bullied at Bradford, yes as a 'sprog' (rookie), the first one on Blue watch for nine years, I was the brunt of many practical jokes, but as a 26-year-old with some life experience I realised you let them have their fun and it soon passed. I did hear stories of bullying from the 1970s, particularly after 1974 when all the city fire brigades merged and became West Yorkshire Fire Service. Tales of 18-year-old recruits sat on the end of their beds at home in tears at the prospect of going to work to be bullied. Bullying should not be tolerated in any setting, including home, school, workplace, or anywhere else. While occasional jokes highlighting personal quirks can be seen as a form of group acceptance, there is no justification for bullying behaviour.

This fact reminds me of two different stories. When I started on Blue watch it soon became apparent that one colleague was as big a Bradford City fan as myself, so we started going to the games together. We would meet up, go to the match carrying out our usual routine, find our regular place on the Kop, this being the new kop rebuilt after the fire in 1985. At one game we were stood staring at the pitch waiting for the players to enter the gladiatorial arena when he turned to me and said,

"What's up with you today? You're a bit quiet."

"Oh nothing, it's just the shift are wearing me down a bit." The watch wasn't annoying me actually; I just said that to answer his question quickly. What followed struck a chord which stayed with me throughout my career and beyond.

"Why is that getting to you?" he continued.

"It gets annoying and wearing after some time."

Then he said, and here's the point,

"Right, how much stick do they give…" and he mentioned another colleague's name.

"None! He gets nothing, I get it all," I answered.

"Exactly, they hate his guts, whereas you are one of the team and are accepted to be, so just remember in a daft sort of way they love you for it!"

I stood there looking at the pitch for a while, digesting his wise words; he was right, the micky taking, jokes and tricks (similar to 'The long Stand' at Leeds University) were never done with any malice, it was all done in good humour and to be honest was a sign of acceptance. The pranks and jokes I was the brunt of as a young firefighter never felt like I was being bullied, and I am convinced that it was never intended as bullying. It was all high jinks and great humour which makes the world go round, all of which made the job, teamwork and camaraderie fantastic and appealing.

My next tale on this subject illustrates the change in times and thoughts throughout my firefighting career. I had been in the Service about 20 years and the Brigade decided because of attitude change in society each employee would attend an Equal Opportunities and Diversity course. This involved one day in a classroom at training school being made aware of this relatively new subject. In my opinion, it was an excellent initiative to educate staff on respecting and understanding people's differences. I have no problem with this at all, my motto has always been 'live and let live', my explanation of this statement is let people do and believe what they want in their lives as long as it's legal and it doesn't interfere with my life as I can do with my life what I want, it's called FREEDOM! I attended the course, which aimed to raise awareness among me and my colleagues about racism, misogyny, sexuality, and bullying, all of which are important topics.

There were about a dozen fire service employees of various ranks on the course. In the morning, we discussed race and gender. After dinner, we returned to discuss bullying and sexuality. During my tenure in the fire service, there were numerous instances of high jinks, practical jokes, humour, and teasing, none of which I would classify as bullying. I wished to convey this perspective to the instructors and the rest of the class. So, with a slight mischievous intention I put my hand up and the following conversation took place.

"Yes, Andy, what would you like to say?" asked the instructor as she noticed my raised hand.

"I think you have a difficult task on your hands with this subject because I feel there is a fine line between bullying and banter, and this job is built on banter," I replied.

"I totally agree with you," she said. "Our office is full of healthy banter."

So I went for the punchline,

"Yes! Because until I joined this job, I never realised how small, fat and ugly I actually am!"

Crescendo! The whole class were in stitches, laughing, whooping, cheering and banging desks. Objective achieved; I was making a point in what I hoped was a very funny way to which I got the reaction I was after from the rest of the class. Hang on a minute, this is where my misjudgement hit me between the eyes. As my colleagues were guffawing, the instructor stared straight into my eyes, never once did she glance elsewhere as she held an emotionless look on her face which was quite unnerving. Then as the raucous noise subsided to an uncomfortable silence, she enquired in a monotone voice,

"That's awful, Andy, and has that ever bothered you?"

'Bothered me? Bothered me? Did she not understand?' The firefighters I had worked with over the previous 20 years referred to me as the small, fat, ugly rat due to me being short, overweight and ugly, a description I embraced as I considered it to be a term of endearment.

"No!" I replied with slight disdain. "I just believe it to indicate acceptance within my working group."

At this she turned away and continued with the rest of the lesson.

Nothing else was said about my intervention until the end of the day's instruction. After the class was dismissed, I was asked to stay back for a minute as the instructor wanted to have a word with me. She told me she had concerns about what I had said, and if I wanted to take it further, she would be willing to do so on my behalf. Not at all, I explained it had no detrimental effect on me whatsoever and I accepted it in the humour I firmly believed it was delivered with. I made it clear I considered it to be a term of endearment at which point I left believing the instructor didn't really understand.

In conclusion, I never experienced any bullying in my time as a firefighter, although I was the brunt of many a trick and practical joke which in my mind was all part of the job. Nothing was ever done or said with malice and if on the rare occasion a wind up was going too far the perpetrators would quickly back off. Everyone was in it for the common goal, to save life and property, with all the jokes and wind ups made the shift and team a more together and happier group. One last thought: people suggest banter is another word for bullying whereas I believe people who don't get the joke blame banter as bullying. I understand different people think and behave in different ways, but have we really come to a point where we can't have a laugh for fear of offending someone. Finally, does this mean the TV shows like Candid Camera, Beagles About, The Gocha Oscars and Ant and Dec are all bullying their victims? I think not!!!